# AMERICA

## STATE BY STATE

AMERICA STATE BY STATE

HarperCollins books may be purchased for educational, business,
or sales promotional use. For information please e-mail the
Special Markets Department at SPsales@harpercollins.com.

First published in 2017 by
Harper Design
An Imprint of HarperCollinsPublishers
195 Broadway
New York, NY 10007
Tel: (212) 207-7000
Fax: (855) 746-6023
www.hc.com
harperdesign@harpercollins.com

Distributed throughout the world by
HarperCollinsPublishers
195 Broadway
New York, NY 10007

ISBN 978-0-06-257167-0

Printed in China
First Printing, 2017

# AMERICA
## STATE BY STATE

### FIFTY REMOVABLE PLACEMATS TO COLOR

Holly Graham

HARPER
DESIGN

An Imprint of HarperCollins Publishers

"For a map of Washington, DC, that can be downloaded and printed for coloring, please visit hc.com/dcmap."

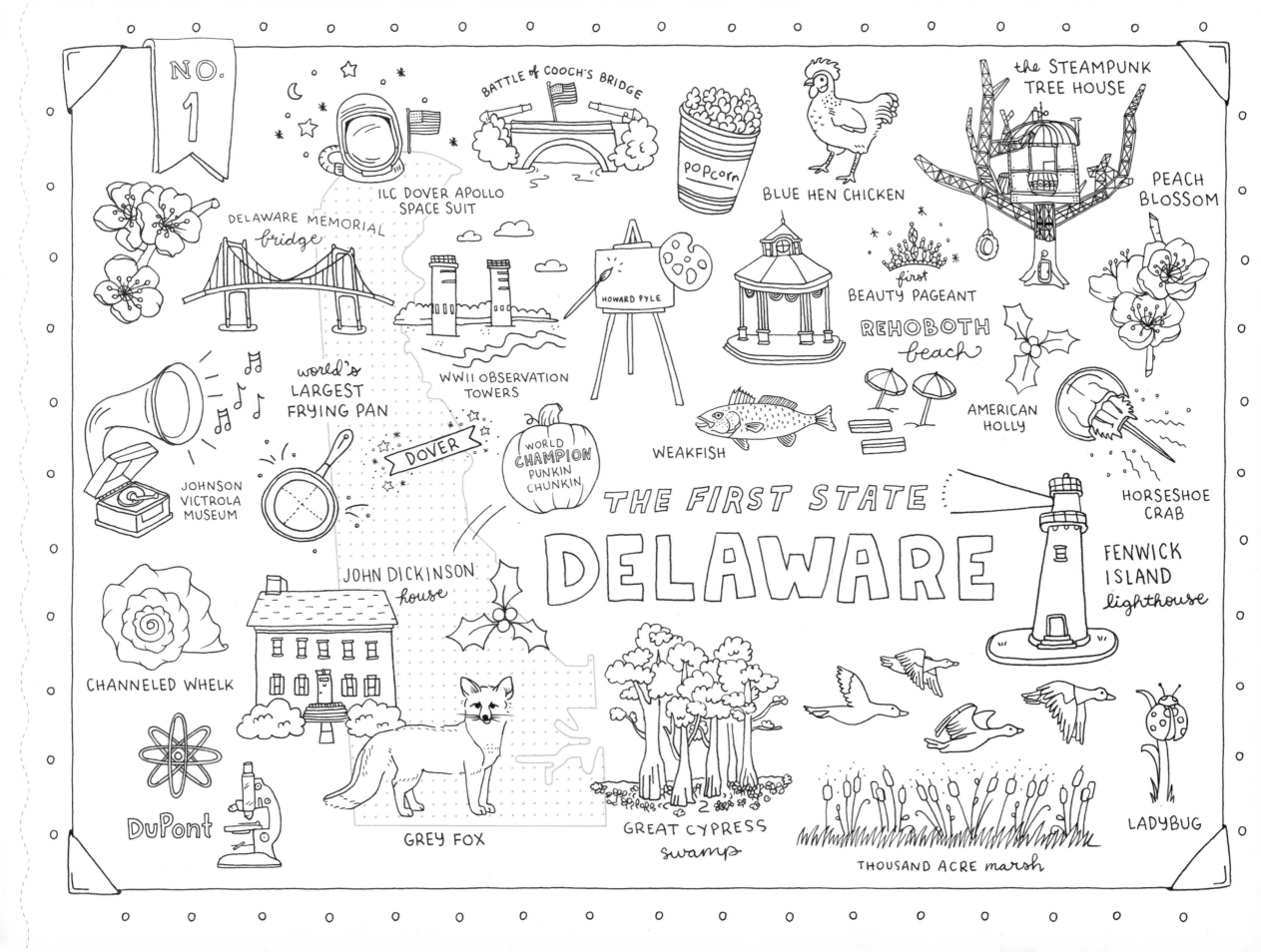

# DELAWARE

1ST STATE

*(entered the Union on December 7, 1787)*

**Capital:** Dover

**Nicknames:** The First State,
   The Diamond State,
   Blue Hen State,
   Small Wonder

**Motto:** "Liberty and Independence"

### STATE SYMBOLS

**Animal (wildlife):** grey fox
**Animal (marine):** horseshoe crab
**Bird:** blue hen chicken
**Fish:** weakfish
**Flower:** peach blossom
**Insect:** ladybug
**Seashell:** channeled whelk
**Tree:** American holly

### LANDMARKS AND PLACES OF INTEREST

Delaware Memorial Bridge
John Dickinson House
Johnson Victrola Museum
Battle of Cooch's Bridge
Rehoboth Beach
Fenwick Island Lighthouse
The Steampunk Tree House
Great Cypress Swamp
Thousand Acre Marsh
World's Largest Frying Pan
World War II observation towers

### TRADITIONS AND EVENTS

World Championship Punkin Chunkin

### PEOPLE

Howard Pyle

### FAMOUS FIRSTS

highly mobile space suit (Apollo A7LB)
beauty pageant (held at Rehoboth Beach)

### INDUSTRY

DuPont

# PENNSYLVANIA

2ᴺᴰ STATE

*(entered the Union on December 12, 1787)*

**Capital:** Harrisburg

**Nickname:** The Keystone State

**Motto:** "Virtue, Liberty, and Independence"

## STATE SYMBOLS

**Animal:** white-tailed deer

**Bird:** ruffed grouse

**Fish:** brook trout

**Flower:** mountain laurel

**Insect:** firefly

**Tree:** hemlock

## LANDMARKS AND PLACES OF INTEREST

Gettysburg

Fallingwater

Rockville Bridge

Liberty Bell

Philadelphia Zoo

Drake Well Museum

"fork" in the road (Centerport, PA)

Rockville Bridge

The Declaration of Independence

Philadelphia Museum of Art

Monongahela and Duquesne Inclines

Phipps Conservatory and Botanical Gardens

"Electric City" (Scranton, PA)

"Switzerland of America" (Jim Thorpe, PA)

## TRADITIONS AND EVENTS

sports teams (Pittsburgh Steelers, Penguins, Pirates; Philadelphia Eagles, Flyers, Phillies)

Punxsutawney Phil

## PEOPLE

William Penn

Andrew Carnegie

Henry Clay Frick

Andy Warhol

Jimmy Stewart

## INVENTIONS

lightning rod

ketchup

banana split

cheesesteak

scrapple

Philly-style soft pretzel

Slinky

## FAMOUS FIRSTS

American flag

piano (in the US)

Ferris wheel

emoticons

## CULTURAL CONTRIBUTIONS

*Rocky*

## INDUSTRY

Hershey's

Crayola

Snack Belt

Martin Guitar

Just Born (Peeps)

# new Jersey

3ʳᵈ STATE

*(entered the Union on December 18, 1787)*

**Capital:** Trenton
**Nickname:** The Garden State
**Motto:** "Liberty and Prosperity"

## STATE SYMBOLS

**Animal:** horse
**Bird:** Eastern goldfinch
**Dinosaur:** hadrosaurus
**Fish:** brook trout
**Flower:** violet
**Insect:** honeybee
**Seashell:** knobbed whelk
**Tree:** red oak

## LANDMARKS AND PLACES OF INTEREST

George Washington Bridge
Atlantic City
Lucy the Elephant
Ellis Island *(see also New York)*
Jersey Shore
Camden Children's Garden
Camden Aquarium
Rainbow Tunnel
Union Water Sphere
Sandy Hook Lighthouse
Asbury Park carousel
Cape May
classic diners

## PEOPLE

Thomas Edison
Frank Sinatra
Bruce Springsteen
Jon Bon Jovi

## INVENTIONS

motion picture
Band-Aid
zipper
Bubble Wrap
bar code
Taylor Ham

## FAMOUS FIRSTS

organized baseball game
drive-in movie theater
salt water taffy
submarine

## CULTURAL CONTRIBUTIONS

books of Judy Blume

## INDUSTRY

Campbell Soup Company
crops (blueberries, cranberries, spinach, bell peppers, peaches, Jersey tomatoes)

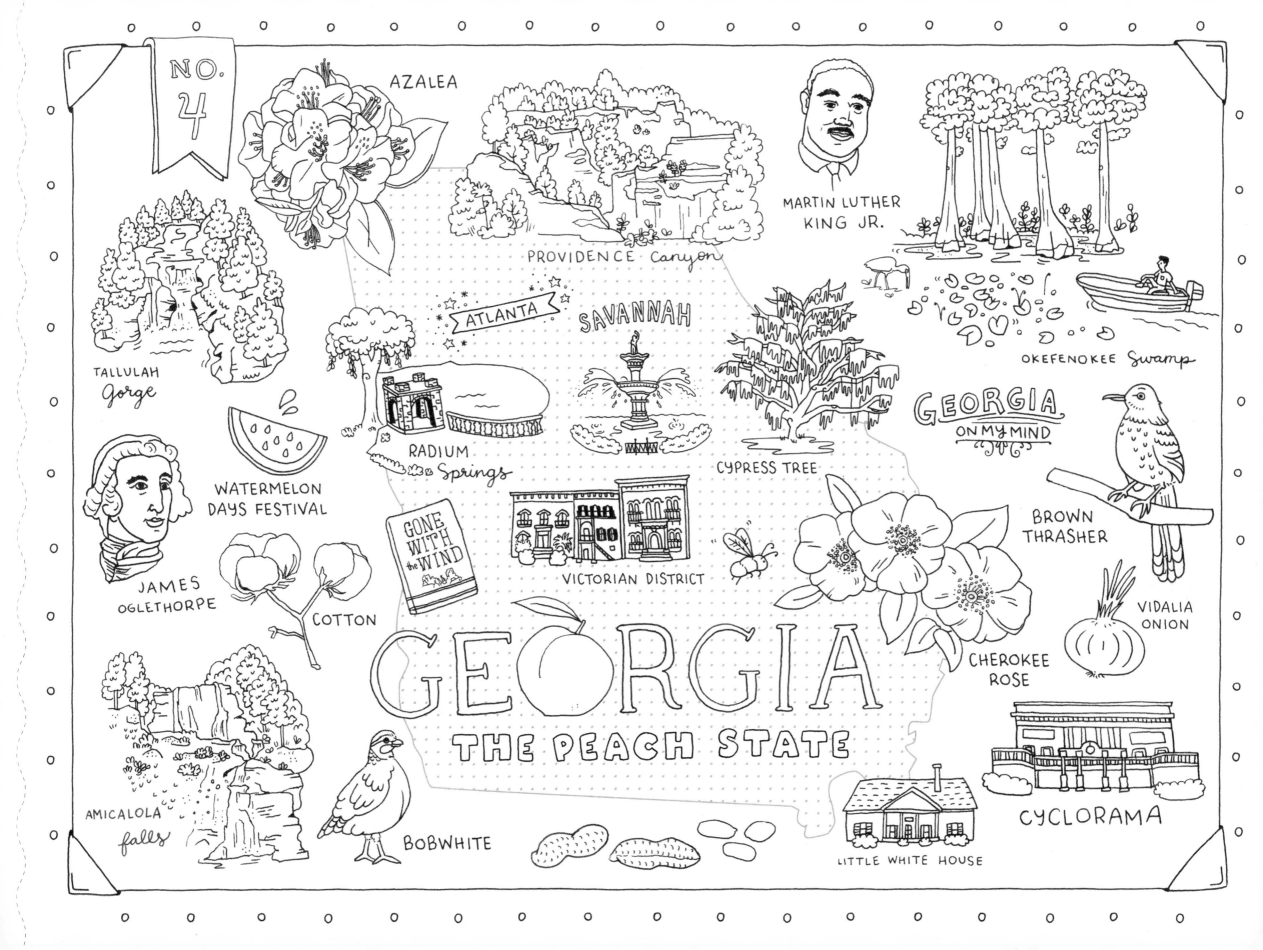

# GEORGIA

4TH STATE

*(entered the Union on January 2, 1788)*

**Capital:** Atlanta

**Nicknames:** The Peach State,
   The Goober State,
   Empire State of the South

**Motto:** "Wisdom, Justice, Moderation"

## STATE SYMBOLS

**Bird:** brown thrasher

**Fish:** largemouth bass

**Flower:** Cherokee rose

**Game bird:** bobwhite

**Insect:** honeybee

**Tree:** live oak

**Wildflower:** azalea

## LANDMARKS AND PLACES OF INTEREST

Tallulah Gorge

Amicalola Falls

Providence Canyon

Savannah

Little White House

Radium Springs

Okefenokee Swamp

Cyclorama

Stone Mountain

The Varsity

Cumberland Island

## TRADITIONS AND EVENTS

Watermelon Days Festival

## PEOPLE

Martin Luther King Jr.

James Oglethorpe (founder)

## INVENTIONS

Coca-Cola

## FAMOUS FIRSTS

24-hour news network (CNN)

## CULTURAL CONTRIBUTIONS

*Gone with the Wind* by Margaret Mitchell

"Georgia on My Mind"

## INDUSTRY

crops (peaches, peanuts, Vidalia onions)

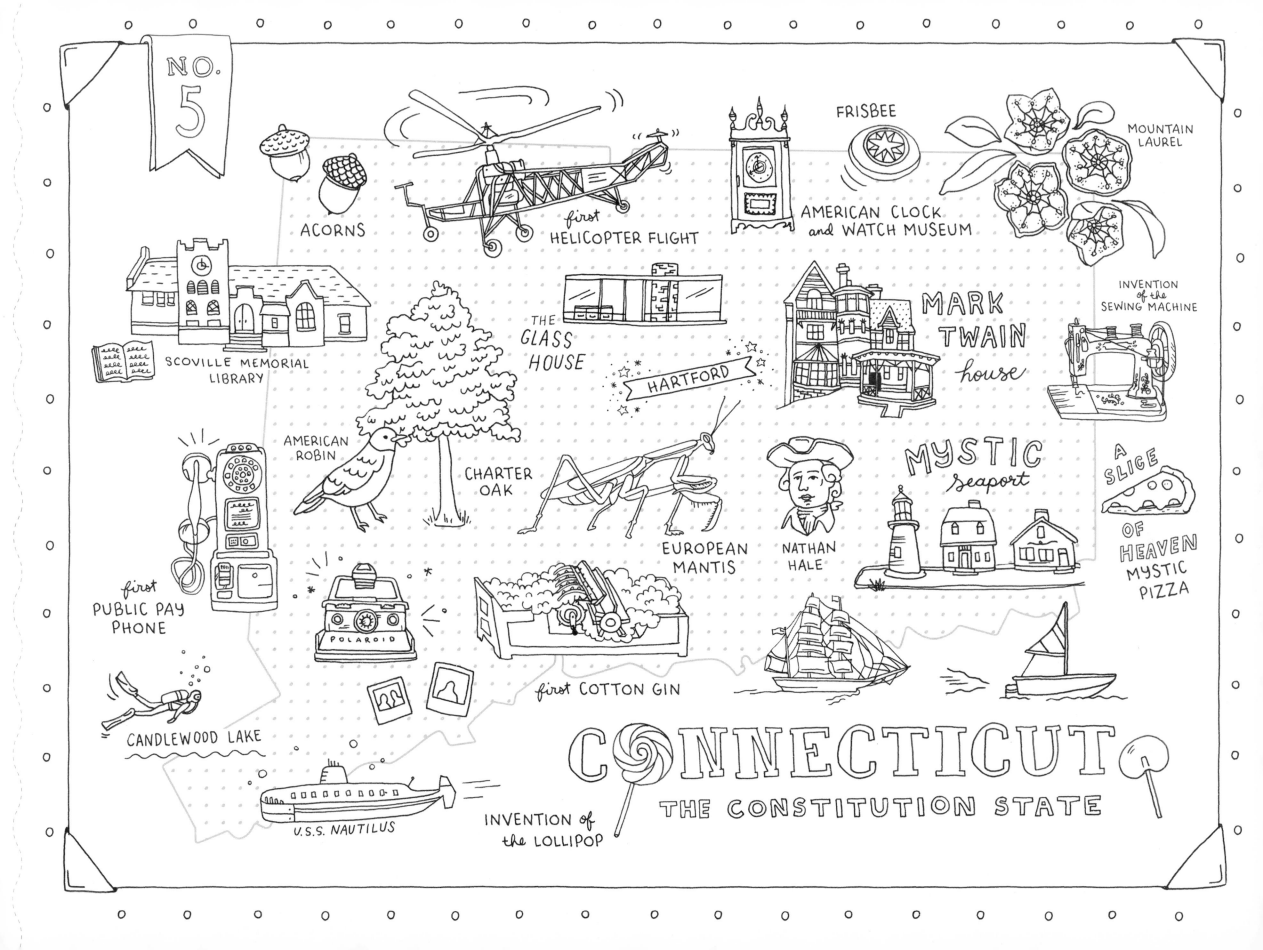

# CONNECTICUT

5TH STATE

*(entered the Union on January 9, 1788)*

**Capital:** Hartford

**Nicknames:** The Constitution State,
The Nutmeg State,
The Land of Steady Habits

**Motto:** "Qui Transtulit Sustenet"
("He Who Transplanted Still Sustains")

## STATE SYMBOLS

**Animal:** sperm whale

**Bird:** American robin

**Fish:** American shad

**Flower:** mountain laurel

**Insect:** European mantis

**Tree:** charter oak

## LANDMARKS AND PLACES OF INTEREST

Scoville Memorial Library

Mystic Seaport

Mystic Pizza

Mark Twain House

Candlewood Lake

The Glass House

USS Nautilus

Yale University

PEZ Visitor Center

Wadsworth Atheneum Museum of Art

## PEOPLE

Nathan Hale

Katharine Hepburn

## INVENTIONS

sewing machine

Polaroid camera

Frisbee

hamburger sandwich

lollipop

## FAMOUS FIRSTS

cotton gin

public pay phone

helicopter flight

woman to receive a US Patent (Mary Kies)

telephone exchange and phone book

automobile law (speed limit of 12 mph)

commercial FM radio station

# Massachusetts

6ᵀᴴ STATE

*(entered the Union on February 6, 1788)*

**Capital:** Boston

**Nicknames:** The Bay State,
The Old Colony State,
The Puritan State,
The Baked Bean State

**Motto:** "Ense Petit Placidam
sub Libertate Quietem"
("By the Sword We Seek Peace,
but Peace Only under Liberty")

## STATE SYMBOLS

**Bean:** navy bean
**Bird:** black-capped chickadee
**Cat:** tabby
**Cookie:** chocolate chip cookie
**Dessert:** Boston cream pie
**Dog:** Boston terrier
**Fish:** cod
**Flower:** mayflower
**Insect:** two-spotted lady beetle
**Muffin:** corn muffin
**Cookie:** chocolate chip cookie

**Bean:** navy bean
**Tree:** American elm

## LANDMARKS AND PLACES OF INTEREST

Old Ship Church
Fenway Park
Martha's Vineyard
Nantucket
Plymouth Rock
Cape Cod National Seashore
Boston Children's Museum
Walden Pond
Salem Witch Trials Memorial
Boston Common

## PEOPLE

Benjamin Franklin
Emily Dickinson
Dr. Seuss (Theodore Geisel)
Johnny Appleseed

## INVENTIONS

basketball (invented by James Naismith)
volleyball (invented by William Morgan)
Marshmallow Fluff
Fig Newtons
plastic pink flamingo

## FAMOUS FIRSTS

Thanksgiving
digital computer (Project Whirlwind)
subway system (in the US)
Dunkin' Donuts shop

## CULTURAL CONTRIBUTIONS

Cheers

## INDUSTRY

seafood

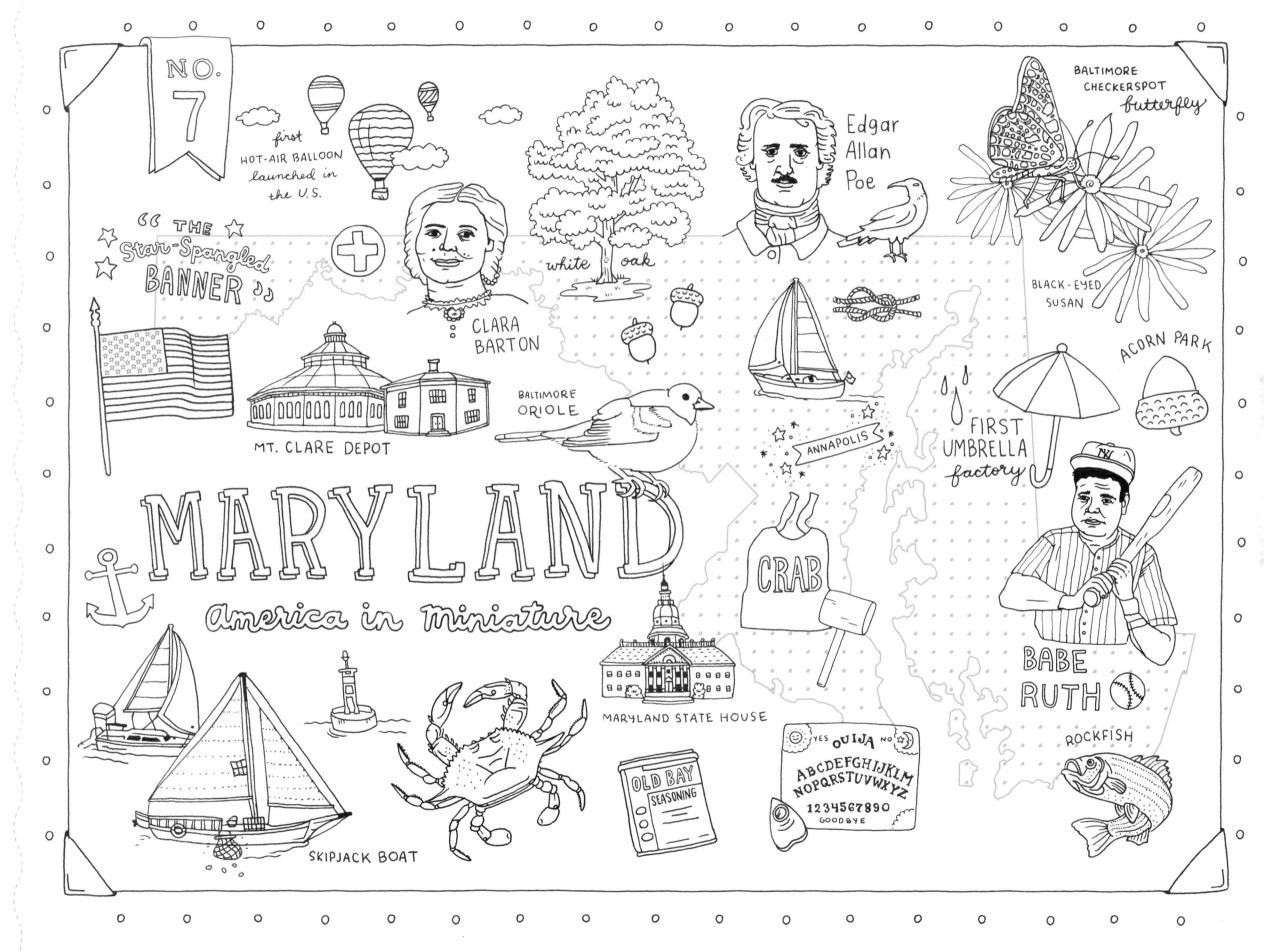

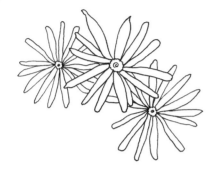

# MARYLAND

## 7TH STATE

*(entered the Union on April 28, 1788)*

**Capital:** Annapolis

**Nicknames:** America in Miniature, The Old Line State, The Free State

**Motto:** "Fatti Maschi Parole Femine" ("Strong Deeds, Gentle Words")

### STATE SYMBOLS

**Bird:** Baltimore oriole

**Cat:** calico

**Crustacean:** Maryland blue crab

**Fish:** rockfish

**Flower:** black-eyed Susan

**Insect:** Baltimore checkerspot butterfly

**Sport:** jousting

**Tree:** white oak

### LANDMARKS AND PLACES OF INTEREST

Mt. Clare depot

Maryland State House

Acorn Park

Fort McHenry

### TRADITIONS AND EVENTS

sports teams (Baltimore Orioles, Ravens)

crab boil

### PEOPLE

Edgar Allan Poe

Clara Barton

Babe Ruth

### INVENTIONS

Ouija board

skipjack boat

### FAMOUS FIRSTS

hot-air balloon launched (in the US)

umbrella factory (in the US)

### CULTURAL CONTRIBUTIONS

"The Star-Spangled Banner" by Francis Scott Key

### INDUSTRY

seafood (crabs, oysters)

Old Bay Seasoning

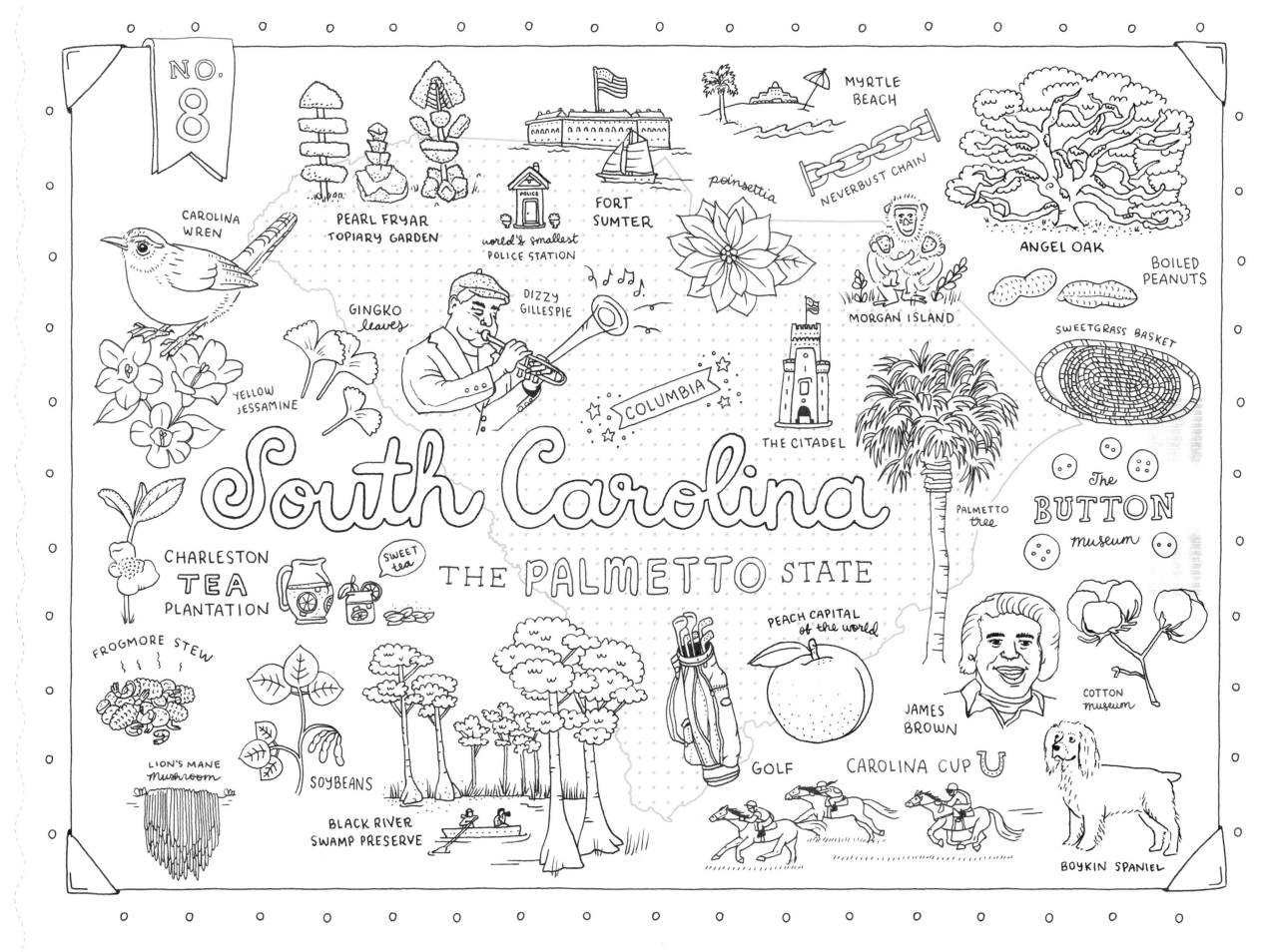

# South Carolina

8TH STATE

*(entered the Union on May 23, 1788)*

**Capital:** Columbia

**Nickname:** The Palmetto State,
Nothing Could Be Finer

**Mottos:** "Animis Opibusque Parati"
("Prepared in Mind and Resources"),
"Dum Spiro Spero"
("While I Breathe I Hope")

## STATE SYMBOLS

**Animal:** white-tailed deer

**Bird:** Carolina wren

**Butterfly:** Eastern tiger swallowtail

**Dog:** Boykin spaniel

**Fish:** striped bass

**Flower:** yellow jessamine

**Insect:** Carolina mantis

**Snack:** boiled peanuts

**Tree:** palmetto

## LANDMARKS AND PLACES OF INTEREST

Black River Swamp Preserve

Neverbust Chain

Cotton Museum

Myrtle Beach

Pearl Fryar Topiary Garden

Angel Oak

Fort Sumter

The Citadel

Morgan Island

Charleston Tea Plantation

The Button Museum

world's largest commercial gingko farm
(Sumter, SC)

Drayton Hall

Peach Capital of the World (Johnston, SC)

World's Smallest Police Station (Ridgeway, SC)

## TRADITIONS AND EVENTS

Carolina Cup

## PEOPLE

Dizzy Gillespie

James Brown

Clayton "Peg Leg" Bates

## INVENTIONS

Frogmore Stew

shag (dance)

## FAMOUS FIRSTS

poinsettia (in the US)

## CULTURAL CONTRIBUTIONS

sweetgrass basket

## INDUSTRY

crops (soybeans)

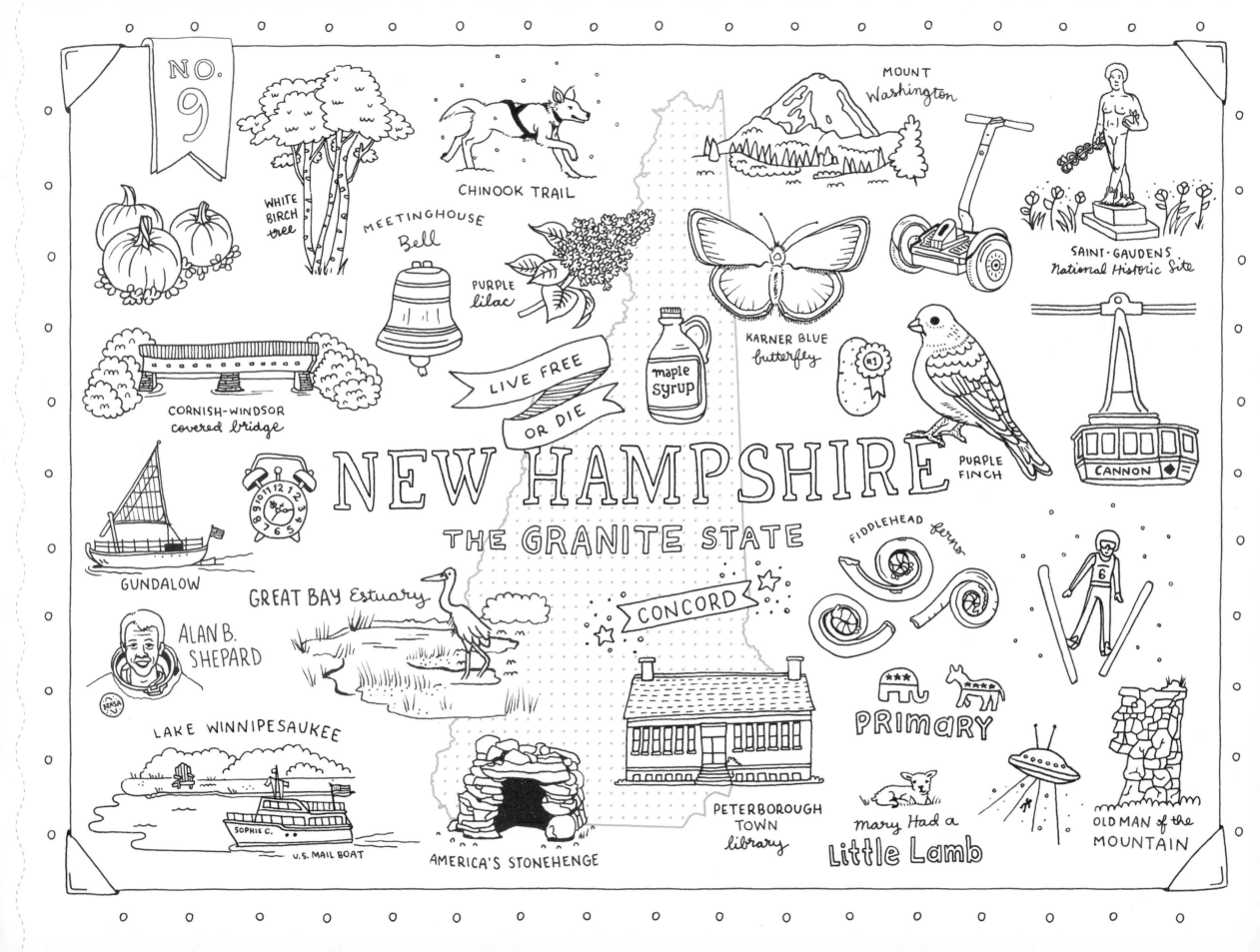

NO. 9

WHITE BIRCH tree

CHINOOK TRAIL

MEETINGHOUSE Bell

PURPLE lilac

MOUNT Washington

SAINT-GAUDENS National Historic Site

KARNER BLUE butterfly

CORNISH-WINDSOR covered bridge

LIVE FREE OR DIE

maple syrup

#1

PURPLE FINCH

CANNON

GUNDALOW

NEW HAMPSHIRE

THE GRANITE STATE

FIDDLEHEAD ferns

ALAN B. SHEPARD

NASA

GREAT BAY Estuary

CONCORD

PRIMARY

LAKE WINNIPESAUKEE

SOPHIE C.

U.S. MAIL BOAT

AMERICA'S STONEHENGE

PETERBOROUGH TOWN library

Mary Had a Little Lamb

OLD MAN of the MOUNTAIN

# NEW HAMPSHIRE

## 9TH STATE

*(entered the Union on June 21, 1788)*

**Capital:** Concord

**Nicknames:** The Granite State,
Mother of Rivers,
The White Mountain State,
Switzerland of America

**Motto:** "Live Free or Die"

### STATE SYMBOLS

**Amphibian:** red-spotted newt

**Animal:** white-tailed deer

**Bird:** purple finch

**Butterfly:** Karner blue butterfly

**Fish (freshwater):** brook trout

**Fish (saltwater):** striped bass

**Flower:** purple lilac

**Fruit:** pumpkin

**Insect:** ladybug

**Tree:** white birch

**Wildflower:** pink lady's slipper

### LANDMARKS AND PLACES OF INTEREST

Meetinghouse Bell

Cornish-Windsor Covered Bridge

Chinook Trail

Mount Washington

*Sophie C.* on Lake Winnipesaukee
(oldest floating post office in the US)

Great Bay Estuary

Old Man of the Mountain

Saint-Gaudens National Historical Site

Cannon Mountain Aerial Tramway

America's Stonehenge

### TRADITIONS AND EVENTS

New Hampshire primary

### PEOPLE

Alan B. Shepard

### INVENTIONS

alarm clock

Segway and Luke bionic arm
(both made by DEKA)

### FAMOUS FIRSTS

free public library
(Peterborough Town Library)

potato planted (in the US)

widely publicized claim of an alien
abduction (Betty and Barney Hill)

### CULTURAL CONTRIBUTIONS

"Mary Had a Little Lamb"

NO. 10

CHESAPEAKE BAY BRIDGE - TUNNEL

BLUE RIDGE Mountains

"GIVE ME Liberty OR GIVE ME Death"

dogwood

MOUNT VERNON

CHESAPEAKE BAY

OLD DOMINION

THE PENTAGON

VIRGINIA

THOMAS JEFFERSON

ELLA FITZGERALD

VIRGINIA is for Lovers

ASSATEAGUE Island

RICHMOND

Cardinal

COLONIAL WILLIAMSBURG

RICHMOND UNION PASSENGER RAILWAY

EAST & WEST END LINE

PRESIDENTIAL PET MUSEUM

ARLINGTON NATIONAL CEMETERY

CRABTREE falls

GREAT DISMAL Swamp

CHINCOTEAGUE PONY SWIM

SPUDNUTS

AMERICAN FOXHOUND

Smithfield HAM

# VIRGINIA

10TH STATE

*(entered the Union on June 25, 1788)*

**Capital:** Richmond

**Nicknames:** Old Dominion,
Mother of States

**Motto:** "Sic Semper Tyrannus"
("Thus Always to Tyrants")

## STATE SYMBOLS

**Bird:** cardinal

**Dog:** American foxhound

**Fish:** brook trout

**Flower:** dogwood

**Insect:** tiger swallowtail butterfly

**Tree:** dogwood

## AND PLACES OF INTEREST

Colonial Williamsburg

Chesapeake Bay

Blue Ridge Mountains
*(see also North Carolina)*

The Pentagon

Chesapeake Bay Bridge-Tunnel

Assateague Island

Mount Vernon

Arlington National Cemetery

Crabtree Falls

Presidential Pet Museum

Great Dismal Swamp

## TRADITIONS AND EVENTS

Chincoteague Pony Swim

## PEOPLE

Thomas Jefferson

Patrick Henry

Ella Fitzgerald

## INVENTIONS

Spudnut

## FAMOUS FIRSTS

Richmond Union Passenger
Railway (first successful electric
street railway in the world)

## INDUSTRY

Seafood (oysters, crabs)

Smithfield hams

winemaking

# New York

## 11TH STATE

*(entered the Union on July 26, 1788)*

**Capital:** Albany

**Nickname:** The Empire State

**Motto:** "Excelsior" ("Ever Upward")

### STATE SYMBOLS

**Animal:** beaver

**Bird:** bluebird

**Fish:** brook trout

**Flower:** rose

**Fruit:** apple

**Insect:** ladybug

**Tree:** sugar maple

### LANDMARKS AND PLACES OF INTEREST

Niagara Falls

Coney Island

Empire State Building

Guggenheim Museum

Broadway

Chinatown

Catskill Mountains

Woodstock

Adirondack Mountains

Statue of Liberty

Ellis Island *(see also New Jersey)*

Chrysler Building

Hudson River

Kykuit (the Rockefeller Estate)

Brooklyn Bridge

Erie Canal

The Gunks

Women's Rights National Historical Park

Lake George

### TRADITIONS AND EVENTS

Saranac Lake Winter Carnival

### PEOPLE

Sojourner Truth

Jackie Robinson

Elizabeth Cady Stanton

### INVENTIONS

commercial toilet paper

potato chips

Buffalo wings

ready-made mayonnaise

Thousand Island dressing

### FAMOUS FIRSTS

ice cream sundae (debatable; see Illinois and Wisconsin)

women's rights convention (Seneca Falls Convention)

pizzeria in the US (Lombardi's)

to require cars to have license plates

### CULTURAL CONTRIBUTIONS

"The Legend of Sleepy Hollow" by Washington Irving

Harlem Renaissance

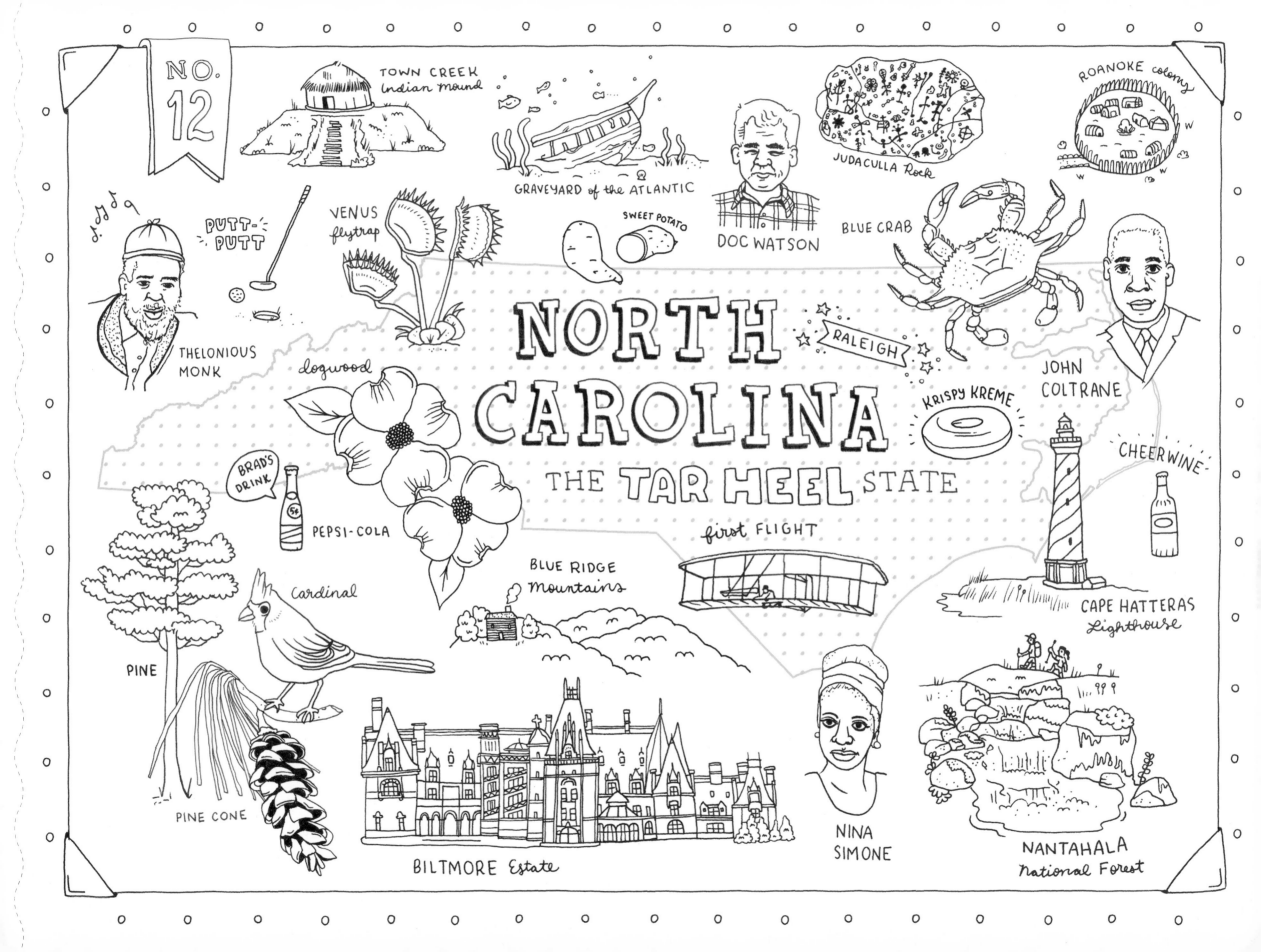

# NORTH CAROLINA

12ᵀᴴ STATE

*(entered the Union on November 21, 1789)*

**Capital:** Raleigh

**Nicknames:** The Tar Heel State,
The Old North State, First in Flight

**Motto:** "Esse Quam Videri"
("To Be Rather Than to Seem")

## STATE SYMBOLS

**Bird:** cardinal

**Butterfly:** Eastern tiger swallowtail

**Carnivorous plant:** Venus flytrap

**Fish:** channel bass

**Flower:** dogwood

**Insect:** honeybee

**Mammal:** gray squirrel

**Tree:** pine

**Vegetable:** sweet potato

## LANDMARKS AND PLACES OF INTEREST

Blue Ridge Mountains *(see also Virginia)*

Cape Hatteras Lighthouse

Town Creek Indian Mound

Biltmore Estate

Graveyard of the Atlantic (the Outer Banks)

Nantahala National Forest

Roanoke Colony

Judaculla Rock

Research Triangle

Great Smoky Mountains National Park
*(see also Tennessee)*

## TRADITIONS AND EVENTS

college basketball (Duke and UNC at Chapel Hill)

## PEOPLE

Nina Simone

Doc Watson

John Coltrane

Thelonius Monk

## INVENTIONS

Pepsi-Cola (originally called Brad's
Drink for its creator Caleb Bradham)

Cheerwine

Putt-Putt

chowchow

## FAMOUS FIRSTS

flight (Wright brothers)

Krispy Kreme donuts

## WILDLIFE

Banker horses

## INDUSTRY

Research Triangle

furniture

tobacco

textiles

brick

Christmas trees

Seafood (blue crabs)

# RHODE ISLAND

13TH STATE

*(entered the Union on May 29, 1790)*

**Capital:** Providence

**Nicknames:** The Ocean State, The Plantation State, The Smallest State, Little Rhody

**Motto:** "Hope"

## STATE SYMBOLS

**Bird:** Rhode Island red

**Fish:** striped bass

**Flower:** violet

**Shell:** quahog

**Tree:** red maple

## LANDMARKS AND PLACES OF INTEREST

Block Island

Slater Mill Historic Site

Cogswell Tower

Flying Horse Carousel
(oldest carousel in the U.S.)

White Horse Tavern
(oldest operating tavern in the U.S.)

Green Animals Topiary Garden

International Tennis Hall of Fame

Touro Synagogue

"Nibbles Woodaway" (world's largest bug)

*Indomitable* (Kodiak bear sculpture)

St. Mary's Church
(where JFK and Jackie were married)

Brown University

Clingstone

Rose Island Light

Newport mansions

Redwood Library and Athenaeum
(oldest library building and lending library in US)

## TRADITIONS AND EVENTS

WaterFire Providence

Newport Folk Festival

Newport Jazz Festival

## PEOPLE

H.P. Lovecraft

## INVENTIONS

Quonset hut

coffee milk

stuffies (stuffed quahog clams)

## FAMOUS FIRSTS

diner

circus

torpedo boat (USS *Stiletto*)

straw hat (in the US)

## CULTURAL CONTRIBUTIONS

RISD

## INDUSTRY

Hasbro

Del's Frozen Lemonade

Narragansett beer

seafood (wild oysters)

# VERMONT

14TH STATE

*(entered the Union on March 4, 1791)*

**Capital:** Montpelier
**Nickname:** The Green Mountain State
**Motto:** "Freedom and Unity"

## STATE SYMBOLS

**Amphibian:** Northern leopard frog
**Animal:** Morgan horse
**Bird:** hermit thrush
**Butterfly:** monarch butterfly
**Flower:** red clover
**Insect:** honeybee
**Tree:** sugar maple

## LANDMARKS AND PLACES OF INTEREST

Lake Champlain
Naulakha (Rudyard Kipling House)
covered bridges
Quechee Gorge
Vermont Teddy Bear Company
"Champ" (Lake Champlain Monster)
Smugglers' Notch
Killington
Ben & Jerry's Flavor Graveyard
The Great Vermont Corn Maze
Chazy Reef

## PEOPLE

Ethan Allen
Calvin Coolidge
Norman Rockwell
Von Trapp family
John Deere

## FAMOUS FIRSTS

postage stamp

## CULTURAL CONTRIBUTIONS

Phish

## INDUSTRY

Ben & Jerry's
Burton
dairy
maple syrup

# KENTUCKY

15TH STATE

*(entered the Union on June 1, 1792)*

**Capital:** Frankfort
**Nickname:** The Bluegrass State
**Motto:** "United We Stand,
    Divided We Fall"

## STATE SYMBOLS

**Bird:** cardinal
**Butterfly:** viceroy butterfly
**Fish:** Kentucky spotted bass
**Flower:** goldenrod
**Music:** bluegrass
**Tree:** tulip poplar

## LANDMARKS AND PLACES OF INTEREST

Cumberland Falls
Abe Lincoln's birthplace
Churchill Downs
Mammoth Cave
Kentucky Speedway
Appalachian Trail
state capitol building
World Peace Bell

## TRADITIONS AND EVENTS

Kentucky Derby
Thunder Over Louisville

## PEOPLE

Daniel Boone
Loretta Lynn
Muhammad Ali
Duncan Hines

## INVENTIONS

radio
the high five
enamel bathtub
hot brown

## FAMOUS FIRSTS

Kentucky Fried Chicken restaurant

## CULTURAL CONTRIBUTIONS

"Happy Birthday to You"
"My Old Kentucky Home"

## INDUSTRY

Louisville Slugger
mirrored balls
bourbon
Corvettes
Post-It Notes

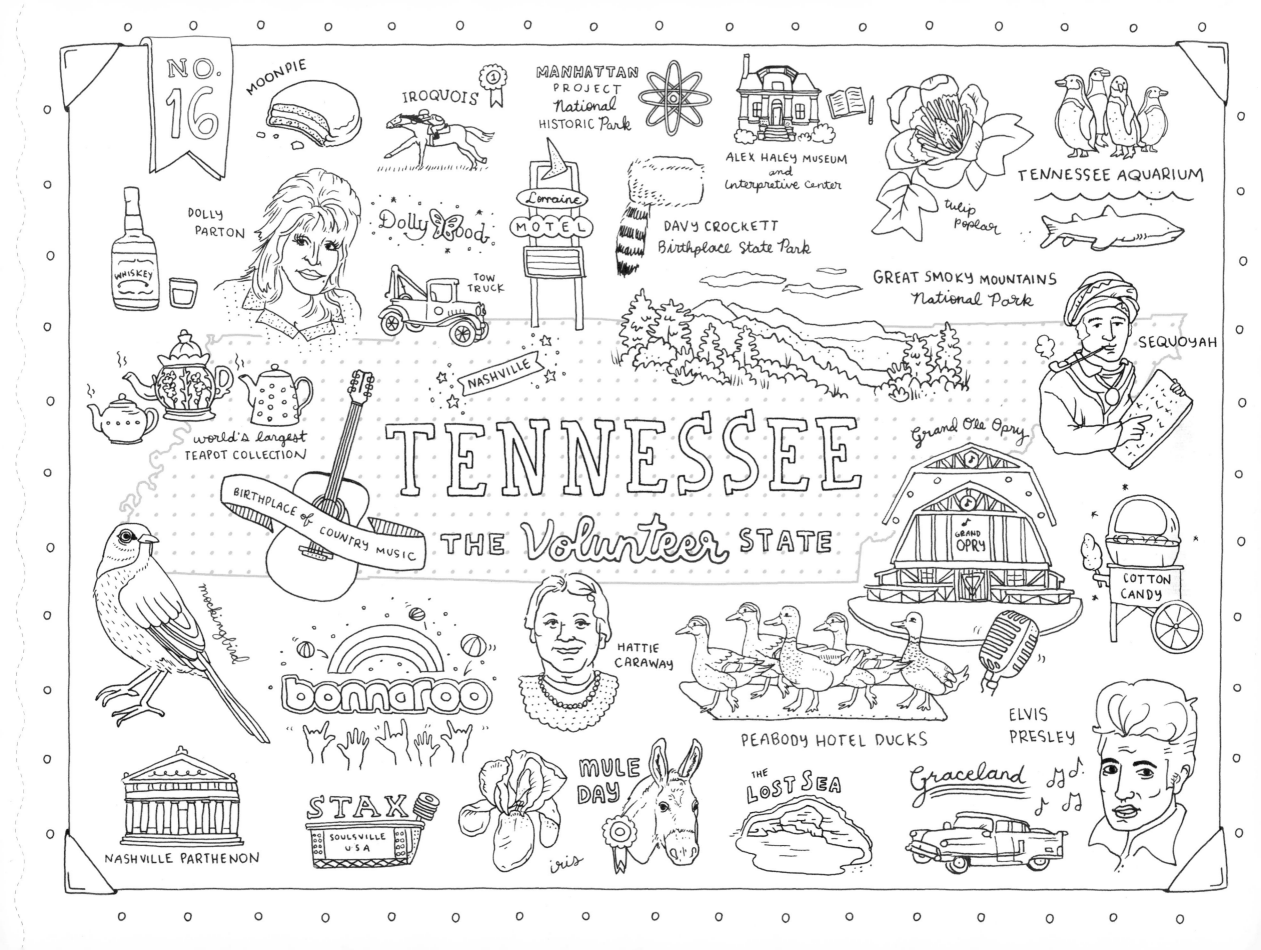

# TENNESSEE

16TH STATE

*(entered the Union on June 1, 1796)*

**Capital:** Nashville

**Nicknames:** The Volunteer State, The Butternut State

**Motto:** "Agriculture and Commerce"

## STATE SYMBOLS

**Animal:** raccoon

**Bird:** mockingbird

**Butterfly:** zebra swallowtail

**Fish:** smallmouth bass (sport fish), channel catfish (commercial fish)

**Flower:** iris

**Insects:** firefly, ladybug, honeybee

**Tree:** tulip poplar

## LANDMARKS AND PLACES OF INTEREST

Great Smoky Mountains National Park
*(see also North Carolina)*

Grand Ole Opry

Birthplace of Country Music (Bristol, TN)

Davy Crockett Birthplace State Park

Alex Haley Museum and Interpretive Center

Graceland

Tennessee Aquarium

World's Largest Teapot Collection

Peabody Hotel ducks

Dollywood

National Civil Rights Museum
at the Lorraine Hotel

Stax Museum of American Soul Music

Nashville Parthenon (in Centennial Park)

The Lost Sea (Craighead Caverns)

Manhattan Project National Historic Park

International Towing & Recovery Museum

## TRADITIONS AND EVENTS

Bonnaroo

Mule Day

## PEOPLE

Dolly Parton

Hattie Caraway (first female US senator)

Sequoyah

## INVENTIONS

tow truck

cotton candy machine

MoonPie

Mountain Dew

## FAMOUS FIRSTS

Iroquois (first American thoroughbred racehorse to win the English Derby)

## CULTURAL CONTRIBUTIONS

country music

## INDUSTRY

whiskey

# OHIO

17TH STATE

*(entered the Union on March 1, 1803)*

**Capital:** Columbus

**Nicknames:** The Buckeye State, The Heart of It All, The Mother of Presidents

**Motto:** "With God, All Things Are Possible"

## STATE SYMBOLS

**Bird:** cardinal

**Flower:** red carnation

**Insect:** ladybug

**Mammal:** white-tailed deer

**Tree:** buckeye

## LANDMARKS AND PLACES OF INTEREST

Hopewell Culture National Park

Serpent Mound

Rock and Roll Hall of Fame

West Side Market

Marblehead Lighthouse

Dave Grohl Alley (world's largest drumsticks)

"House of Trash"

*Field of Corn (with Osage Orange Trees)* aka "Cornhenge"

World's Largest Horseshoe Crab

Cedar Point

Hocking Hills State Park

Cuyahoga Valley National Park

Glacial Grooves Geological Preserve,

"Bessie" (Lake Erie Monster)

National Underground Railroad Freedom Museum

## TRADITIONS AND EVENTS

sports teams (Cleveland Cavaliers, Indians, Browns; Ohio State football; Cincinnati Reds)

Soap Box Derby

Annie Oakley Festival

## PEOPLE

John Glenn

Neil Armstrong

LeBron James

## INVENTIONS

hot dog

Life Savers

pop-top can

golf ball

chewing gum

Cincinnati chili

## FAMOUS FIRSTS

police car

cash register

## CULTURAL CONTRIBUTIONS

Superman

## INDUSTRY

tomato juice (largest producer of)

# LOUISIANA

18TH STATE

*(entered the Union on April 30, 1812)*

**Capital:** Baton Rouge
**Nicknames:** The Pelican State,
  The Bayou State
**Motto:** "Union, Justice, Confidence"

## STATE SYMBOLS

**Bird:** Eastern brown pelican
**Crustacean:** crawfish
**Doughnut:** beignet
**Fish:** white perch
**Flower:** magnolia blossom
**Insect:** honeybee
**Mammal:** black bear
**Reptile:** alligator
**Song:** "You Are My Sunshine"
**Tree:** bald cypress

## LANDMARKS AND PLACES OF INTEREST

Nottoway Plantation House
Superdome
bayou
French Quarter
state capitol building
St. Charles Avenue streetcar
Café du Monde

## TRADITIONS AND EVENTS

Mardi Gras

## PEOPLE

Louis Armstrong

## INVENTIONS

Creole cuisine (gumbo, jambalaya,
  po' boy sandwich)
Sazerac cocktail
binocular microscope

## FAMOUS FIRSTS

opera (in the US)

## PEOPLE

Louis Armstrong

## CULTURAL CONTRIBUTIONS

Dixieland jazz
zydeco

## INDUSTRY

Tabasco
seafood (crawfish, oysters)
Cajun accordians

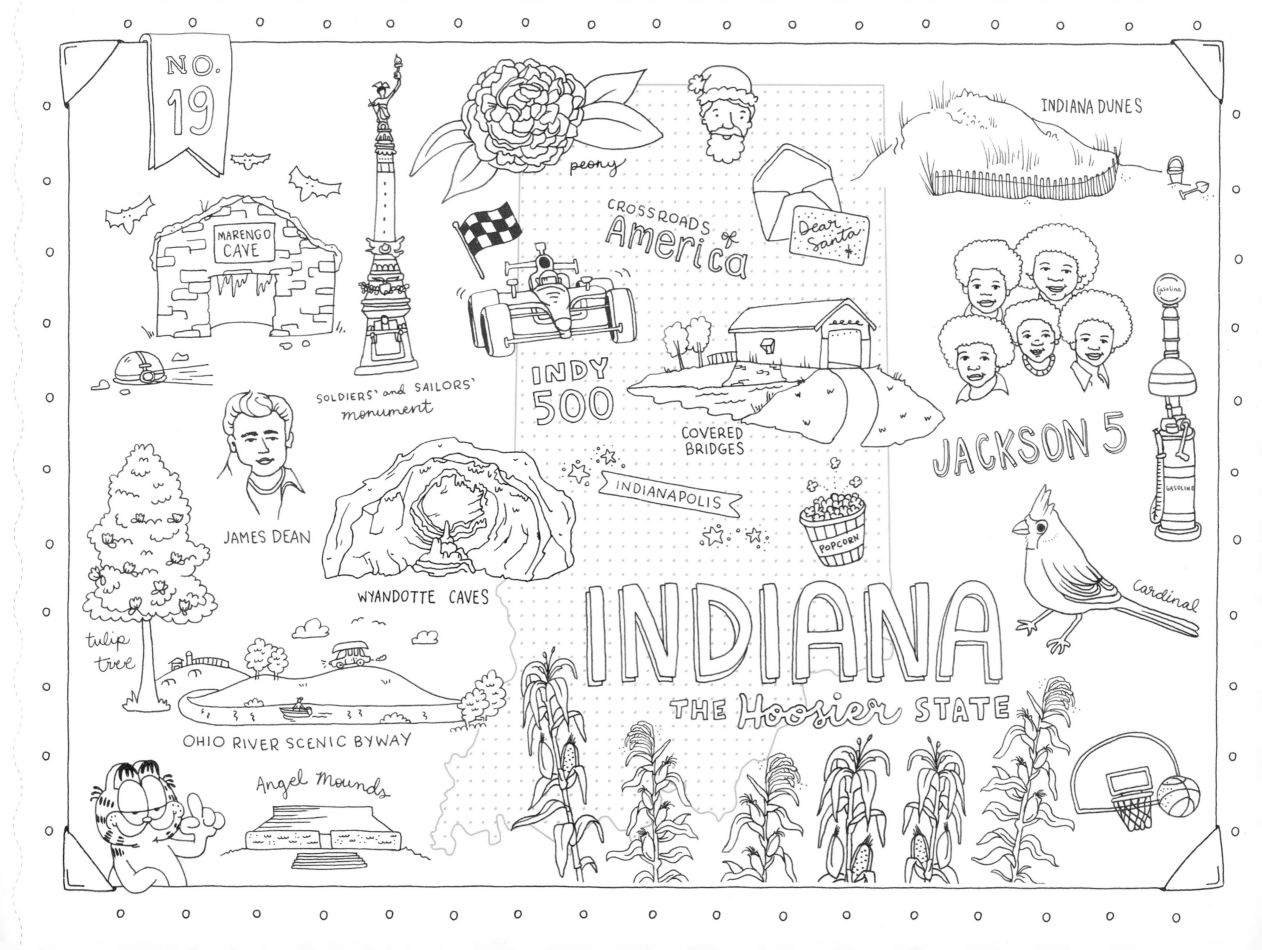

# INDIANA

19TH STATE

*(entered the Union on December 11, 1816)*

**Capital:** Indianapolis
**Nickname:** The Hoosier State
**Motto:** "The Crossroads of America"

## STATE SYMBOLS

**Bird:** cardinal
**Flower:** peony
**Tree:** tulip tree

## LANDMARKS AND PLACES OF INTEREST

Marengo Cave
Soldiers' and Sailors' Monument
Indiana Dunes
Ohio River Scenic Byway
Angel Mounds
Santa Claus, Indiana
Wyandotte Caves
covered bridges
Old Ben (world's largest steer)

## TRADITIONS AND EVENTS

Indianapolis 500
Hoosier basketball

## PEOPLE

Jackson 5
James Dean

## INVENTIONS

gas pump

## CULTURAL CONTRIBUTIONS

*Garfield* by Jim Davis

## INDUSTRY

crops (corn, specifically popcorn)

# MISSISSIPPI

20TH STATE

*(entered the Union on December 10, 1817)*

**Capital:** Jackson

**Nicknames:** The Magnolia State,
The Hospitality State

**Motto:** "Virtute et Armis"
("Valor and Arms")

## STATE SYMBOLS

**Bird:** mockingbird

**Butterfly:** spicebush swallowtail

**Fish:** largemouth bass

**Flower:** magnolia

**Insect:** honeybee

**Mammal (land):** white-tailed deer

**Mammal (water):** bottle-nosed dolphin

**Shell:** oyster

**Tree:** magnolia

## LANDMARKS AND PLACES OF INTEREST

Natchez Trace

world's only cactus plantation

Friendship Cemetery

Biloxi Lighthouse

Old Spanish Fort (has the world's
largest shrimp on display)

Mississippi River

## PEOPLE

Elvis Presley

## INVENTIONS

Barq's Root Beer

## FAMOUS FIRSTS

bottled Coca-Cola

shoes sold in pairs in boxes

"teddy" bear (named for Theodore
"Teddy" Roosevelt after he partook
in a bear hunt in the state)

## CULTURAL CONTRIBUTIONS

blues music

## INDUSTRY

Seafood (shrimp, oysters)

Peavey Electronics

# ILLINOIS

21ST STATE

*(entered the Union on December 3, 1818)*

**Capital:** Springfield

**Nicknames:** The Land of Lincoln,
The Prairie State

**Motto:** "State Sovereignty,
National Union"

## STATE SYMBOLS

**Animal:** white-tailed deer

**Bird:** cardinal

**Fish:** bluegill

**Flower:** violet

**Insect:** monarch butterfly

**Tree:** white oak

## LANDMARKS AND PLACES OF INTEREST

Willis Tower

Shedd Aquarium

Cahokia Mounds State Historic Site

Navy Pier

Metropolis

John Hancock Center

Chicago Water Tower

"The Bean" (*Cloud Gate*)

Route 66 (starts in Chicago)

Frank Lloyd Wright Studio

World's Largest Catsup Bottle

Magnificent Mile

The Wrigley Building

Tribune Tower

## TRADITIONS AND EVENTS

sports teams (Cubs, White Sox,
Bears, Bulls, Blackhawks)

## PEOPLE

Al Capone

Ernest Hemingway

## INVENTIONS

tower silo

Twinkies

deep-dish pizza

Chicago-style hot dogs

ice cream sundae
(This fact is debatable!)

## FAMOUS FIRSTS

13th Amendment
(first state to ratify it)

ice cream sundae (debatable;
see New York and Wisconsin)

skyscraper

## CULTURAL CONTRIBUTIONS

improv comedy (The Second City)

## INDUSTRY

crops (pumpkins, corn, soybeans)

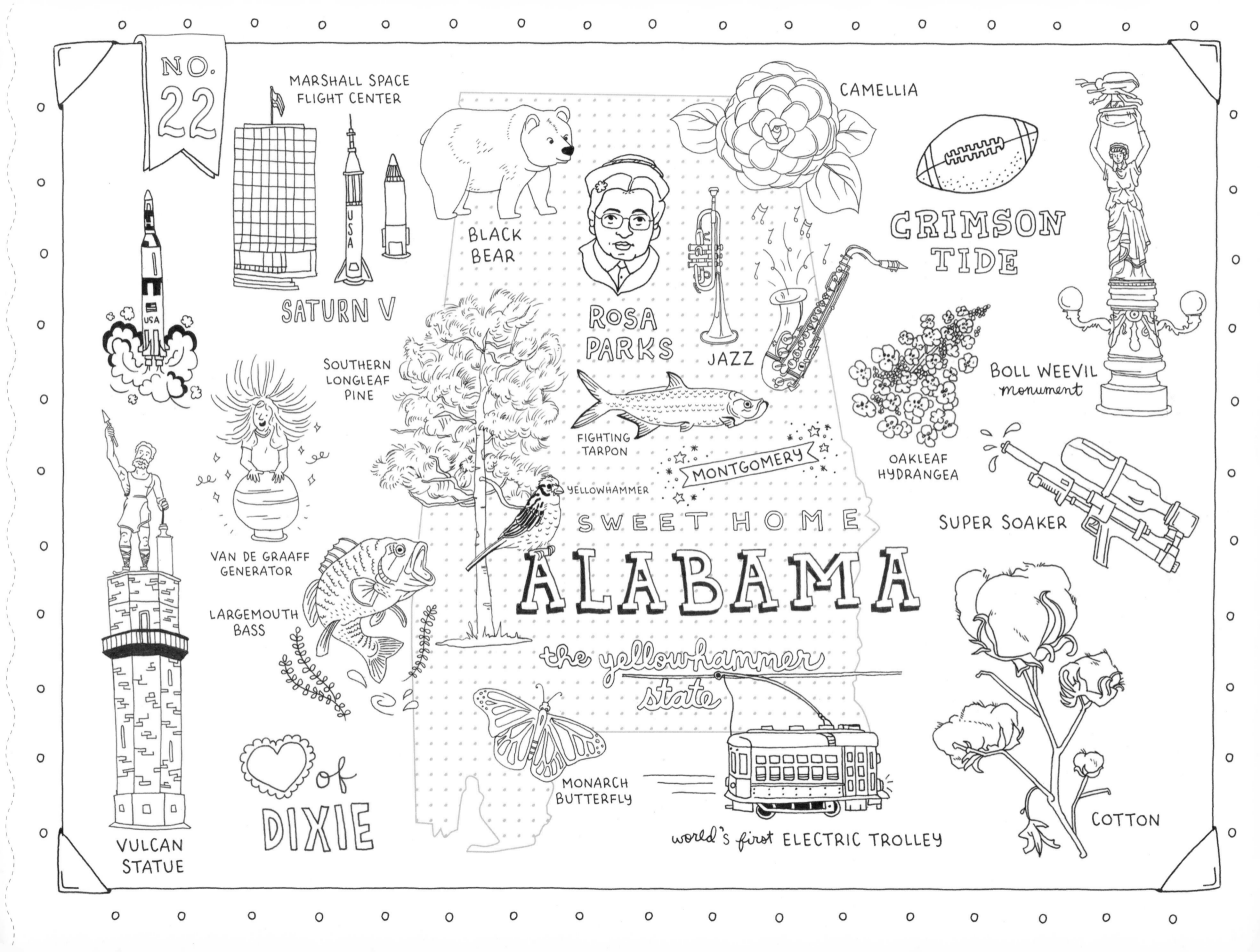

# ALABAMA

## 22ND STATE

*(entered the Union December 14, 1819)*

**Capital:** Montgomery
**Nicknames:** The Yellowhammer State,
 The Heart of Dixie
**Motto:** "Audemus Jura Nostra Defendere"
 ("We Dare Defend Our Rights")

### STATE SYMBOLS

**Bird:** yellowhammer
**Fish (freshwater):** largemouth bass
**Fish (saltwater):** fighting tarpon
**Flower:** camellia
**Insect:** monarch butterfly
**Mammal:** black bear
**Tree:** Southern longleaf pine

### LANDMARKS AND PLACES OF INTEREST

Vulcan Statue
Boll Weevil Monument
Marshall Space Flight Center
Jemison-Van de Graaff Mansion

### TRADITIONS AND EVENTS

Crimson Tide football

### PEOPLE

Rosa Parks
Helen Keller
Nat King Cole
Zelda Fitzgerald

### INVENTIONS

Van de Graaff generator
Super Soaker

### FAMOUS FIRSTS

electric trolley (world's first)

### CULTURAL CONTRIBUTIONS

"Sweet Home Alabama" by Lynyrd Skynyrd
*To Kill a Mockingbird* by Harper Lee
blues and jazz

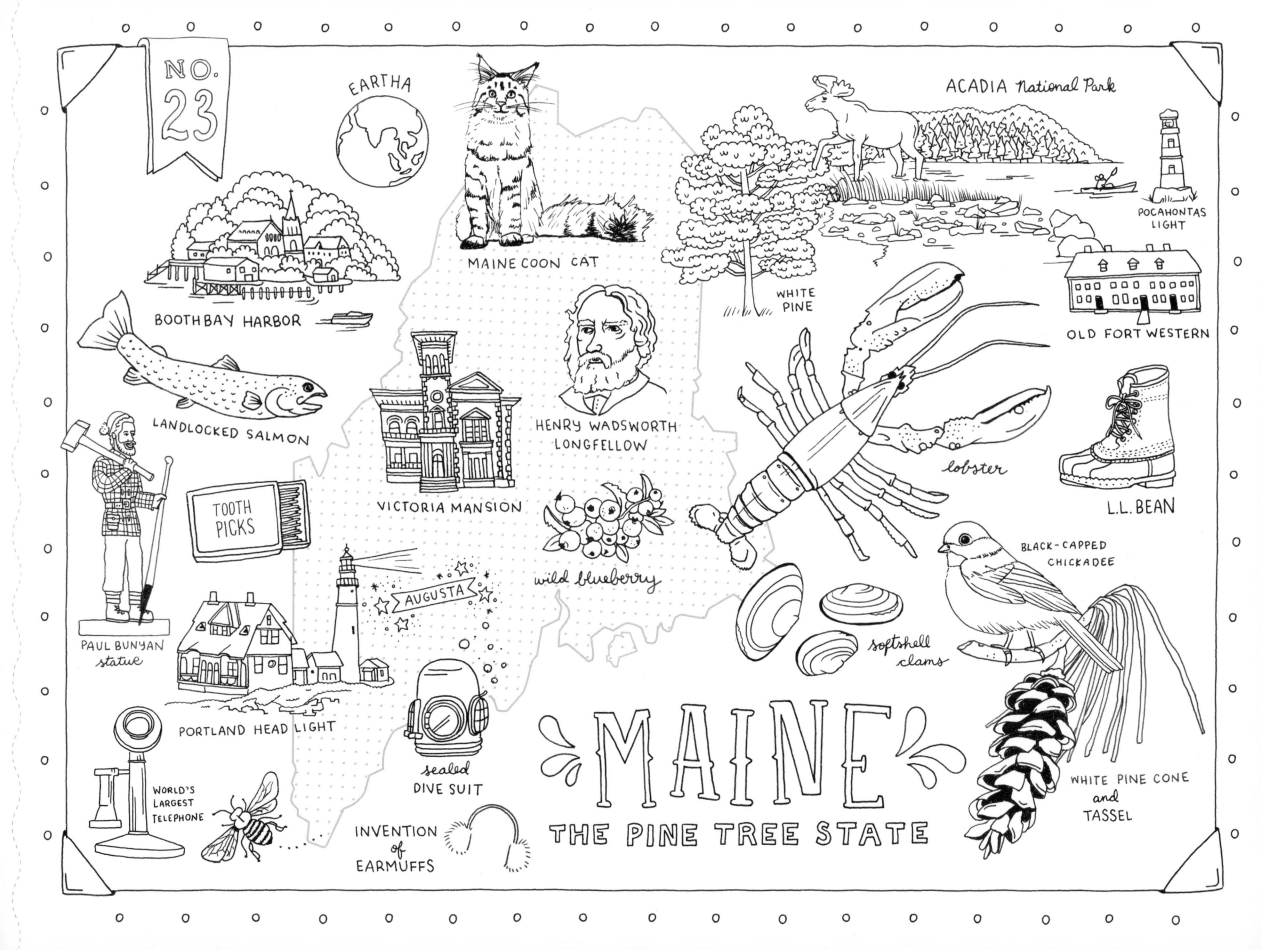

# MAINE

## 23RD STATE

*(entered the Union on March 15, 1820)*

**Capital:** Augusta

**Nicknames:** The Pine Tree State, Vacationland

**Motto:** "Dirigo" ("I Lead")

### STATE SYMBOLS

**Animal:** moose

**Berry:** wild blueberry

**Bird:** black-capped chickadee

**Cat:** Maine coon

**Fish:** landlocked salmon

**Flower:** white pine cone and tassel

**Insect:** honeybee

**Tree:** white pine

### LANDMARKS AND PLACES OF INTEREST

Acadia National Park

Boothbay Harbor

Kennebunkport

Victoria Mansion

Paul Bunyan statue *(see also Minnesota)*

Old Fort Western

Portland Head Light

Eartha

World's Largest Telephone

Pocahontas Light

### PEOPLE

Henry Wadsworth Longfellow

Edna St. Vincent Millay

### INVENTIONS

earmuffs

sealed dive suit

### CULTURAL CONTRIBUTIONS

books of Stephen King

### INDUSTRY

seafood (lobsters, softshell clams)

L.L. Bean

toothpicks (largest producer of)

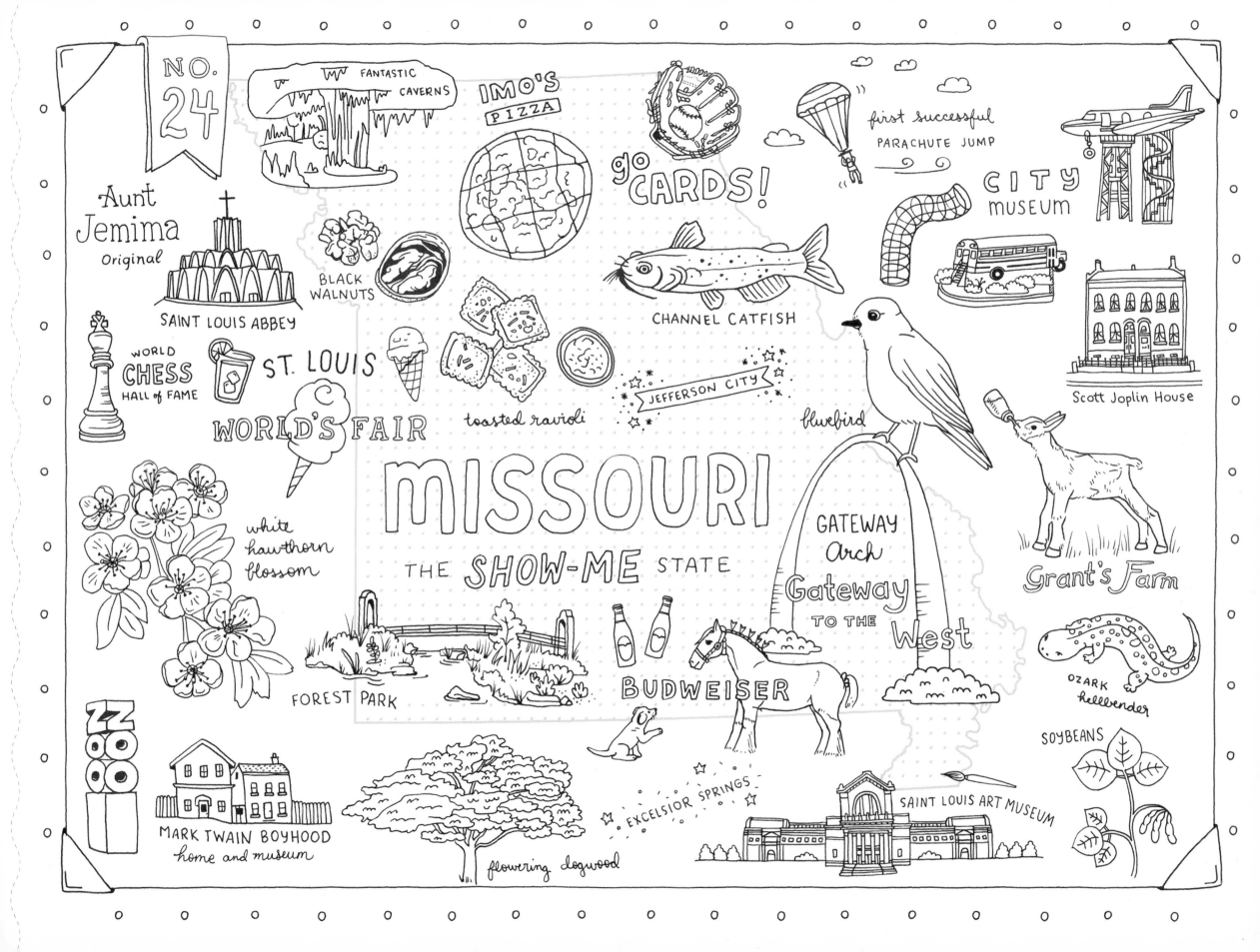

# MISSOURI

24TH STATE

*(entered the Union on August 10, 1821)*

**Capital:** Jefferson City

**Nicknames:** The Show-Me State, Gateway to the West

**Motto:** "Salus Populi Suprema Lex Esto" ("Let the Welfare of the People Be the Supreme Law")

## STATE SYMBOLS

**Animal:** Missouri mule

**Bird:** bluebird

**Fish:** channel catfish

**Flower:** white hawthorn blossom

**Insect:** honeybee

**Tree:** flowering dogwood

## LANDMARKS AND PLACES OF INTEREST

Fantastic Caverns

Saint Louis Abbey

World Chess Hall of Fame

Mark Twain Boyhood Home and Museum

Gateway Arch

City Museum

Saint Louis Zoo

Scott Joplin House

Saint Louis Art Museum

Grant's Farm

Excelsior Springs

Forest Park

Imo's Pizza

Lake of the Ozarks

## TRADITIONS AND EVENTS

St. Louis Cardinals baseball

## PEOPLE

Josephine Baker

## INVENTIONS

toasted ravioli

## FAMOUS FIRSTS

pancake mix (Aunt Jemima)

successful parachute jump

cotton candy, waffle cones, iced tea (introduced at the 1904 St. Louis World's Fair)

## INDUSTRY

Anheuser-Busch

crops (soybeans, black walnuts)

# ARKANSAS

25TH STATE

*(entered the Union on June 15, 1836)*

**Capital:** Little Rock

**Nickname:** The Natural State

**Motto:** "Regnat Populus"
("The People Rule")

### STATE SYMBOLS

**Bird:** mockingbird

**Flower:** apple blossom

**Insect:** honeybee

**Instrument:** fiddle

**Mammal:** white-tailed deer

**Mineral:** quartz crystal

**Nut:** pecan

**Tree:** pine

### LANDMARKS AND PLACES OF INTEREST

Lakeport Plantation

Hot Springs National Park

Thorncrown Chapel

Toltec Mounds State Park

Crater of Diamonds State Park

Wonder Horse

Mount Ida

Eureka Springs

Crystal Bridges Museum of American Art

### TRADITIONS AND EVENTS

Pink Tomato Festival

Arkansas Razorbacks football

### PEOPLE

Johnny Cash

Scott Joplin

General Douglas MacArthur

Freeman Owens

Maya Angelou

### INVENTIONS

Bowie knife

cheese dip

fried pickles

modern archery

### INDUSTRY

archery sets and equipment

duck calls

dulcimers

# MICHIGAN

26TH STATE

*(entered the Union on January 26, 1837)*

**Capital:** Lansing

**Nicknames:** The Wolverine State,
   The Great Lakes State,
   Water Wonderland

**Motto:** "Si Quaeris Peninsulam Amoenam
   Circumspice" ("If You Seek a Pleasant
   Peninsula, Look about You")

## STATE SYMBOLS

**Bird:** robin

**Fish:** brook trout

**Flower:** apple blossom

**Mammal:** white-tailed deer

**Reptile:** painted turtle

**Stone:** Petoskey stone

**Tree:** white pine

**Wildflower:** dwarf lake iris

## LANDMARKS AND PLACES OF INTEREST

Isle Royale National Park

mushroom houses

Mackinac Bridge

Mackinac Island Grand Hotel

Soo Locks

Sleeping Bear Dunes

Detroit

Pictured Rocks National Lakeshore

Cross in the Woods

Il Cavallo dello Sforza

UP (Upper Peninsula)

## TRADITIONS AND EVENTS

Michigan Wolverines football

Tulip Time Festival

Pączki Day

## PEOPLE

Henry Ford

## INVENTIONS

traffic light

fiber optics

ginger ale (Vernors)

## FAMOUS FIRSTS

automotive assembly line

typewriter

road lines

## CULTURAL CONTRIBUTIONS

Motown music

## INDUSTRY

Kellogg's

Gerber

"JIFFY" Mix

crops (cherries, Honeycrisp apples)

# FLORIDA

## 27TH STATE

*(entered the Union on March 3, 1845)*

**Capital:** Tallahassee
**Nickname:** The Sunshine State
**Motto:** "In God We Trust"

### STATE SYMBOLS

**Animal:** Florida panther
**Bird:** mockingbird
**Butterfly:** zebra longwing
**Fish (freshwater):** largemouth bass
**Fish (saltwater):** sailfish
**Flower:** orange blossom
**Mammal (marine):** manatee
**Mammal (saltwater):** dolphin
**Reptile:** American alligator
**Tree:** sabal palm

### LANDMARKS AND PLACES OF INTEREST

Everglades National Park
Disney World
Epcot
Universal Studios
Benwood Shipwreck
The Ringling Circus Museum
Key Largo
Ernest Hemingway House
     (home of polydactyl, or six-toed, cats)
Cape Canaveral
Espiritu Santo Springs
Atlantic Ocean
Gulf of Mexico
Big Cat Rescue

### TRADITIONS AND EVENTS

MLB Spring Training

### PEOPLE

Zora Neale Hurston
Juan Ponce de León (discovered Florida)

### INVENTIONS

suntan lotion
Gatorade

### CULTURAL CONTRIBUTIONS

MiMo (Miami Modernist Architecture)

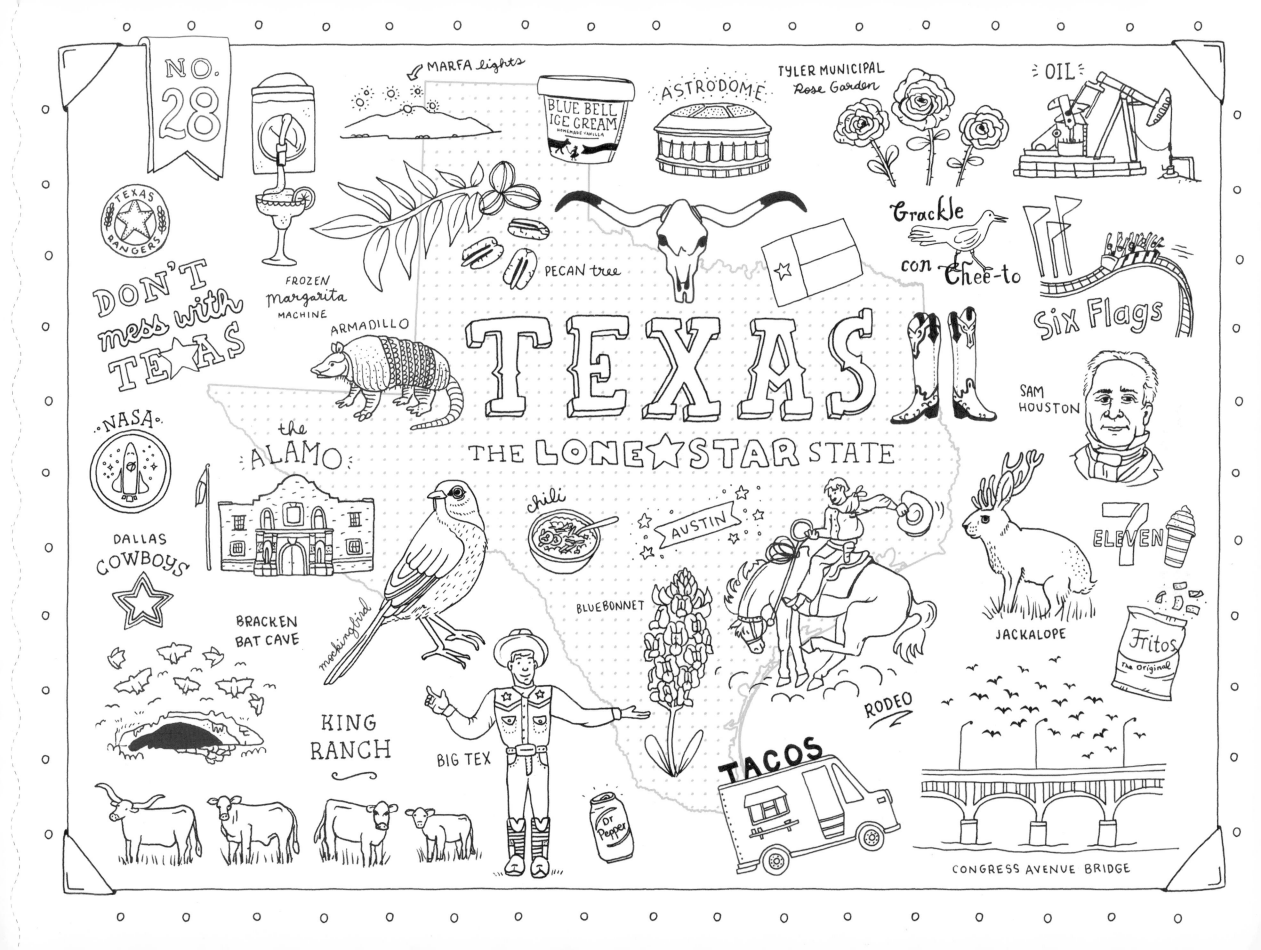

# TEXAS

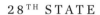

28TH STATE

*(entered the Union on December 29, 1845)*

**Capital:** Austin
**Nickname:** The Lone Star State
**Motto:** "Friendship"

## STATE SYMBOLS

**Bird:** mockingbird
**Dish:** chili
**Fish:** Guadalupe bass
**Flower:** bluebonnet
**Footwear:** cowboy boots
**Insect:** monarch butterfly
**Mammal (large):** longhorn
**Mammal (small):** armadillo
**Tree:** pecan

## LANDMARKS AND PLACES OF INTEREST

Bracken Bat Cave (world's largest bat colony)
The Alamo
Astrodome
Tyler Municipal Rose Garden
Big Tex
Congress Avenue Bridge

## TRADITIONS AND EVENTS

sports teams (Dallas Cowboys,
　　Texas Rangers, Houston Astros)
Marfa lights

## PEOPLE

Sam Houston

## INVENTIONS

Dr Pepper
Fritos
frozen margarita machine

## FAMOUS FIRSTS

rodeo (world's first held in Pecos, TX)
Six Flags theme park
convenience store (world's first;
　　known as 7-Eleven)

## CULTURAL CONTRIBUTIONS

NASA
Grackle con Chee-to

## WILDLIFE

jackalope (notoriously shy
　　whenit comes to photos)

## INDUSTRY

oil
Blue Bell Ice Cream

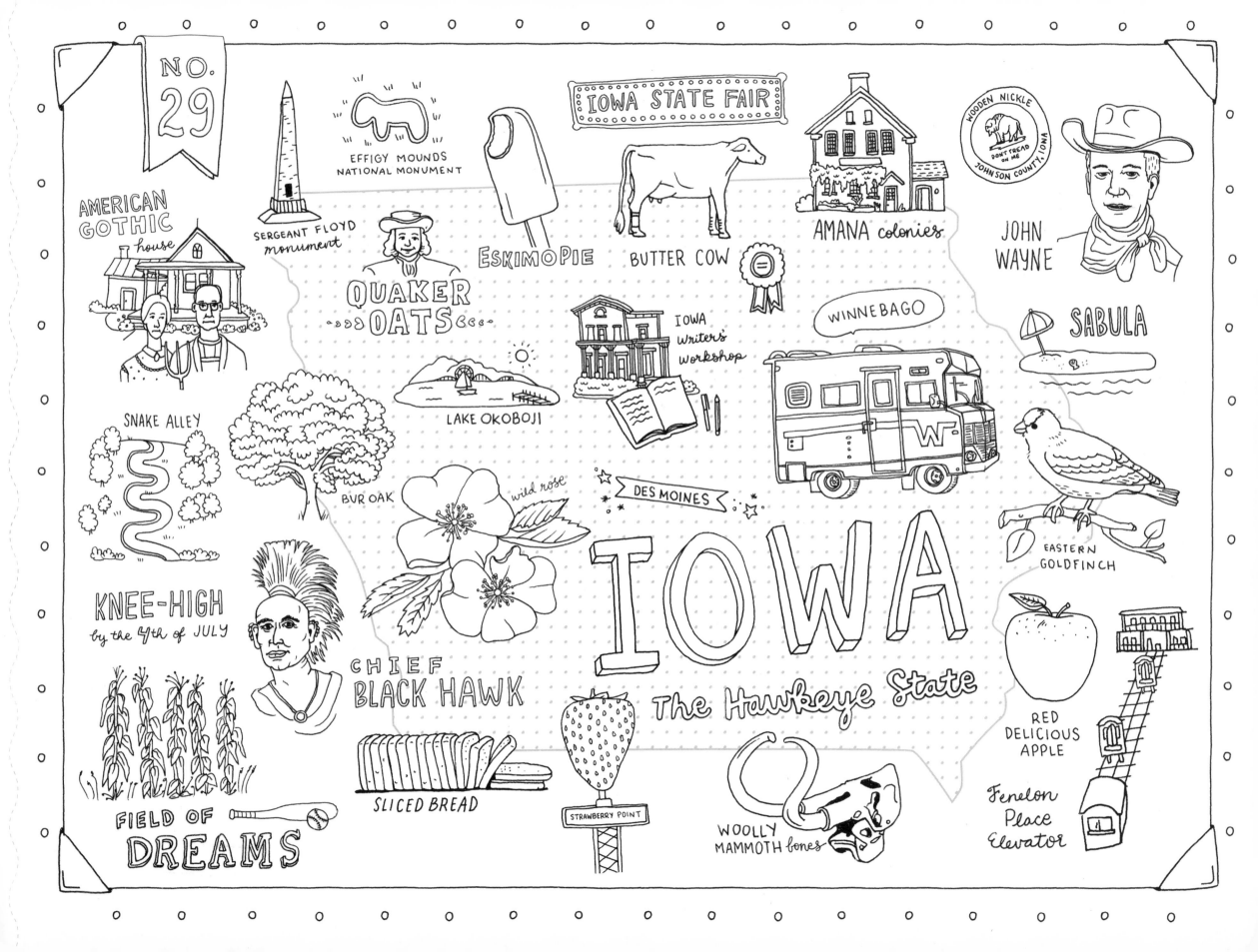

# IOWA

## 29<sup>TH</sup> STATE

*(entered the Union on December 28, 1846)*

**Capital:** Des Moines

**Nickname:** The Hawkeye State

**Motto:** "Our Liberties We Prize,
and Our Rights We Will Maintain"

### STATE SYMBOLS

**Bird:** Eastern goldfinch

**Flower:** wild rose

**Tree:** oak

### LANDMARKS AND PLACES OF INTEREST

Snake Alley

Sergeant Floyd Monument

Lake Okoboji

Amana Colonies

*American Gothic* house

Sabula

World's Largest Wooden Nickel

Effigy Mounds National Monument

Fenelon Place Elevator

Strawberry Point (world's largest strawberry)

Grotto of Redemption

### TRADITIONS AND EVENTS

Iowa State Fair (butter cow)

RAGBRAI

### PEOPLE

Chief Black Hawk

John Wayne

Bix Beiderbecke

### INVENTION

sliced bread (specifically a loaf-at-a-time bread-slicing machine)

Eskimo Pie

### FAMOUS FIRSTS

Red Delicious apples

### CULTURAL CONTRIBUTIONS

Iowa Writers' Workshop

*Field of Dreams*

### INDUSTRY

Winnebago

Quaker Oats

crops and livestock (hogs, eggs, corn)

# WISCONSIN

30TH STATE

*(entered the Union on May 29, 1848)*

**Capital:** Madison

**Nicknames:** The Badger State, The Dairy State, America's Dairyland, The Cheese State

**Motto:** "Forward"

## STATE SYMBOLS

**Animal:** badger

**Bird:** robin

**Fish:** muskellunge

**Flower:** wood violet

**Insect:** honeybee

**Pastry:** kringle

**Tree:** sugar maple

## LANDMARKS AND PLACES OF INTEREST

Wisconsin Dells

Devil's Lake State Park

House on the Rock

Milwaukee Art Museum

Kovac Planetarium

Troll Capital of the World (Mount Horeb, WI)

Taliesin

National Mustard Museum

supper clubs

Toilet Paper Capital of the World (Green Bay, WI)

Door County

Freshwater Fishing Hall of Fame and Museum

## TRADITIONS AND EVENTS

football teams (Green Bay Packers, Wisconsin Badgers)

Summerfest

## PEOPLE

Barbie

## INVENTIONS

blender

QWERTY keyboard layout

ice cream sundae (debatable; see Illinois and New York)

Wisconsin cheese curds

## CULTURAL CONTRIBUTIONS

The Onion

## WILDLIFE

hodags (folkloric creatures)

## INDUSTRY

dairy

crops (cranberries, ginseng)

# CALIFORNIA

31ST STATE

*(entered the Union on September 9, 1850)*

**Capital:** Sacramento
**Nickname:** The Golden State
**Motto:** "Eureka"

### STATE SYMBOLS

**Animal:** grizzly bear
**Bird:** valley quail
**Fish:** golden trout
**Flower:** poppy
**Insect:** California dogface butterfly
**Tree:** California redwood

### LANDMARKS AND PLACES OF INTEREST

Hollywood (Walk of Fame,
    Grauman's Chinese Theatre,
    intersection of Hollywood and Vine)
Joshua Tree National Park
Golden Gate Bridge
Death Valley
Sequoia National Forest
Painted Ladies
Haight-Ashbury
Venice Beach
Disneyland
Mount Whitney
Methuselah
Yosemite National Park
Santa Monica Pier

### INVENTIONS

denim jeans
personal computer
fortune cookies

### FAMOUS FIRSTS

commercial surfboards and skateboards
arcade video game (Pong)

### CULTURAL CONTRIBUTIONS

books of John Steinbeck

### INDUSTRY

Silicon Valley
television and film industry
winemaking
crops (artichokes, avocados,
    almonds, dates)

# MINNESOTA

32ND STATE

*(entered the Union on May 11, 1858)*

**Capital:** Saint Paul

**Nicknames:** The North Star State,
   The Gopher State,
   Land of 10,000 Lakes

**Motto:** "L'Étoile du Nord"
   ("Star of the North")

### STATE SYMBOLS

**Bird:** common loon
**Butterfly:** monarch butterfly
**Fish:** walleye
**Flower:** showy lady's slipper
**Mushroom:** morel
**Tree:** Norway pine

### LANDMARKS AND PLACES OF INTEREST

Split Rock Lighthouse
Minneapolis Skyway
Paul Bunyan statue *(see also Maine)*
Mall of America
Fort Snelling
Minneapolis Sculpture Garden
Boundary Waters Canoe Area
Mary Tyler Moore statue
Bergquist Cabin
Pelican Pete
corn cob gazebo (Olivia, MN)
Old Log Theatre
Aerial Lift Bridge
Lake Itasca (source of the Mississippi River)

### PEOPLE

Bob Dylan
Laura Ingalls Wilder
F. Scott Fitzgerald
Prince

### INVENTIONS

pop-up toaster
automatic stapler
in-line skates
Spam
Bisquick
water skiing

### FAMOUS FIRSTS

"Holy Cow!" expression

### INDUSTRY

3M Company
General Mills

NO. 33

MOUNT HOOD

DOUGLAS FIR

OREGON grape

international ROSE TEST GARDEN

HISTORIC CAROUSEL and MUSEUM

SHANIKO Ghost Town

HELLS CANYON

SALEM

HAYSTACK ROCK

world's largest MUSHROOM

daffodils

THE OREGON TRAIL

LINCOLN CITY'S SUMMER KITE Festival

CHINOOK SALMON

Tillamook Cheese

HACKEY SACK

MILL ENDS Park

hazelnut

OREGON

THE Beaver STATE

WESTERN MEADOWLARK

MULTNOMAH Falls

HECETA HEAD Lighthouse

SEA LION Caves

marionberries

PAINTED HILLS

the SIMPSONS

# OREGON

## 33RD STATE

*(entered the Union on February 14, 1859)*

**Capital:** Salem

**Nicknames:** The Beaver State, Pacific Wonderland

**Motto:** "Alis Volat Propriis" ("She Flies with Her Own Wings")

### STATE SYMBOLS

**Animal:** American beaver

**Bird:** Western meadowlark

**Fish:** Chinook salmon

**Flower:** Oregon grape

**Insect:** Oregon swallowtail

**Nut:** hazelnut

**Tree:** Douglas fir

### LANDMARKS AND PLACES OF INTEREST

Multnomah Falls

Mount Hood

Hells Canyon

International Rose Test Garden

Heceta Head Lighthouse

Painted Hills

Shaniko (ghost town)

Mill Ends Park

Haystack Rock

Historic Carousel & Museum

Tillamook Cheese Factory

Sea Lion Caves

Oregon Trail

Crater Lake National Park

Silver Falls State Park

Oregon Caves National Monument

Tillamook Rock Lighthouse

"D" River (world's shortest river)

Yaquina Head

world's largest mushroom and living organism (a honey fungus that grows underground)

### TRADITIONS AND EVENTS

Lincoln City's Summer Kite Festival

### INVENTIONS

computer mouse

Hacky Sack

marionberry

### CULTURAL CONTRIBUTIONS

*The Simpsons*

*The Goonies*

# KANSAS

34TH STATE

*(entered the Union on January 29, 1861)*

**Capital:** Topeka

**Nicknames:** The Sunflower State, The Jayhawk State, The Wheat State

**Motto:** "Ad Astra Per Aspera" ("To the Stars through Difficulty")

## STATE SYMBOLS

**Animal:** American bison

**Bird:** Western meadowlark

**Flower:** wild native sunflower

**Insect:** honeybee

**Reptile:** ornate box turtle

**Tree:** Eastern cottonwood

## LANDMARKS AND PLACES OF INTEREST

Rock City

Eisenhower boyhood home

Dodge City

John Brown's cabin

Johnny Kaw statue

World's Largest Ball of Twine

## PEOPLE

Amelia Earhart

## INVENTIONS

ICEE

## FAMOUS FIRSTS

patented helicopter

dial telephone

helium (first discovered in Kansas)

## CULTURAL CONTRIBUTIONS

*The Wonderful Wizard of Oz* by L. Frank Baum

"Home on the Range" by Dr. Brewster M. Higley

## WILDLIFE

ruffed grouse

## INDUSTRY

combine harvesters

NO. 35

THE GREENBRIER

MONARCH *butterfly*

SUGAR MAPLE *leaf*

ORGAN CAVE

*Cardinal*

MOTHER'S DAY

WESTON STATE HOSPITAL

RHODODENDRON

GRAVE CREEK *mound*

mountaineers ARE ALWAYS FREE

BLACK BEAR

$ SALES TAX

CHARLESTON

WEST VIRGINIA

THE *Mountain* STATE

JONES DIAMObD

"*Almost Heaven*"

CASS SCENIC *Railroad*

NEW RIVER GORGE BRIDGE

*first* STEAMBOAT

BERKELEY SPRINGS

GREEN BANK *Telescope*

*first* RURAL FREE MAIL DELIVERY

RFD No. 1    U.S. MAIL

COAL HOUSE

NEW RIVER

BROOK TROUT

MOTHMAN

GOLDEN DELICIOUS *apples*

# WEST VIRGINIA

35TH STATE

*(entered the Union on June 20, 1863)*

**Capital:** Charleston

**Nicknames:** The Mountain State,
The Panhandle State,
Switzerland of America

**Motto:** "Montani Semper Liberi"
("Mountaineers Are
Always Free")

## STATE SYMBOLS

**Animal:** black bear
**Bird:** cardinal
**Flower:** rhododendron
**Tree:** sugar maple

## LANDMARKS AND PLACES OF INTEREST

Weston State Hospital
(largest hand-cut stone masonry
building in US)
New River (one of the world's oldest
rivers; runs south to north)
New River Gorge Bridge
Green Bank Telescope
Organ Cave
Coal House
The Greenbrier
Home of the Jones Diamond
(Peterstown, WV)
Mothman statue
Cass Scenic Railroad State Park
Grave Creek Mound

## INVENTIONS

Mother's Day

## FAMOUS FIRSTS

first spa in US (Berkeley Springs, WV)
free rural mail delivery
Golden Delicious apple
(discovered there)
sales tax
steamboat launched
personal rapid transit system

## CULTURAL CONTRIBUTIONS

"Country Roads, Take Me Home"
by John Denver

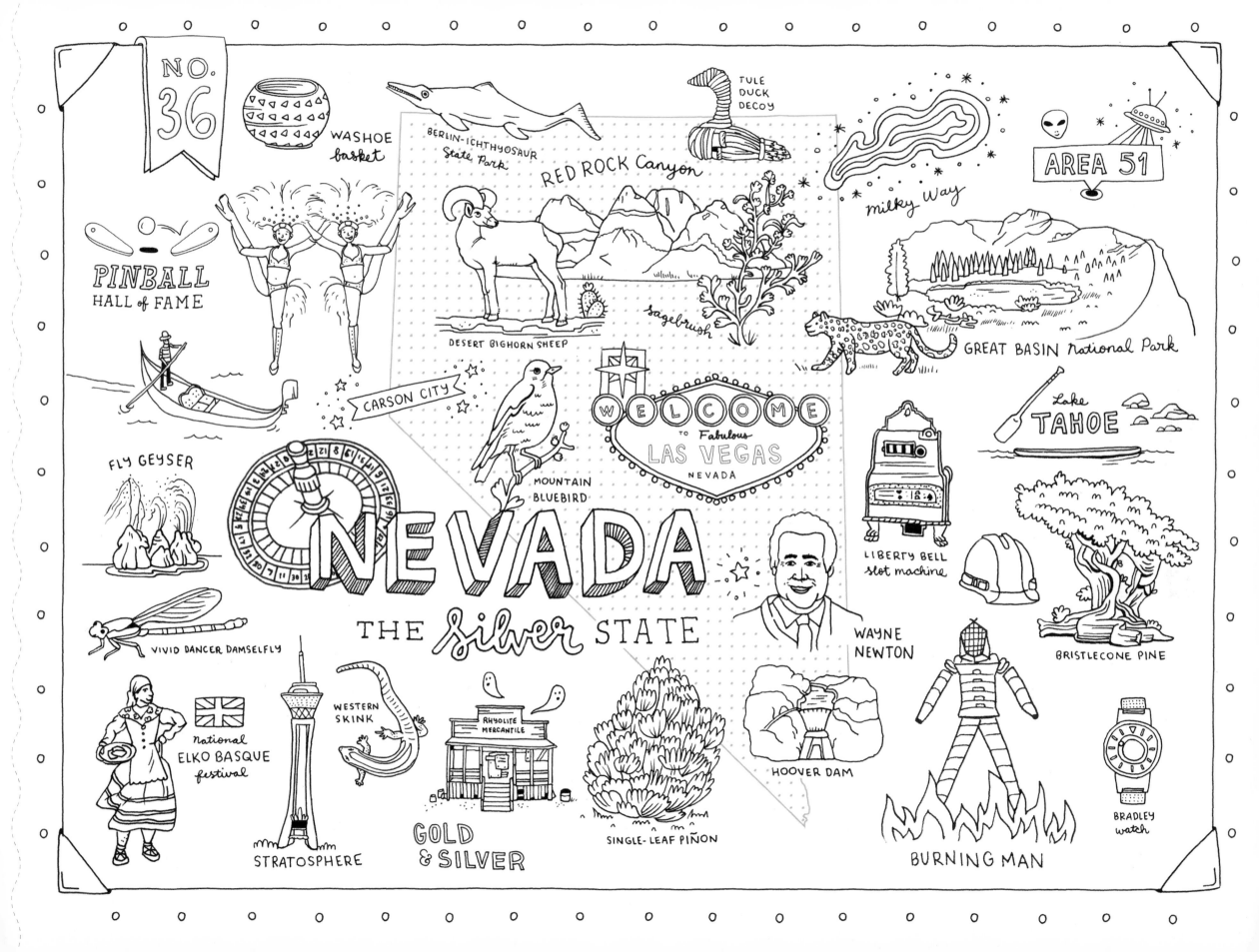

NO. 36

WASHOE basket

BERLIN-ICHTHYOSAUR State Park

TULE DUCK DECOY

RED ROCK Canyon

Milky Way

AREA 51

PINBALL HALL of FAME

DESERT BIGHORN SHEEP

sagebrush

GREAT BASIN national Park

CARSON CITY

WELCOME TO Fabulous LAS VEGAS NEVADA

Lake TAHOE

FLY GEYSER

MOUNTAIN BLUEBIRD

NEVADA

LIBERTY BELL slot machine

VIVID DANCER DAMSELFLY

THE silver STATE

WAYNE NEWTON

BRISTLECONE PINE

national ELKO BASQUE festival

STRATOSPHERE

WESTERN SKINK

RHYOLITE MERCANTILE

GOLD & SILVER

SINGLE-LEAF PIÑON

HOOVER DAM

BURNING MAN

BRADLEY watch

# NEVADA

36TH STATE

*(entered the Union on October 31, 1864)*

**Capital:** Carson City

**Nicknames:** The Silver State,
　　The Sagebrush State

**Motto:** "All for Our Country"

## STATE SYMBOLS

**Animal:** desert bighorn sheep

**Artifact:** tule duck decoy

**Bird:** mountain bluebird

**Fish:** Lahontan cutthroat trout

**Flower:** sagebrush

**Insect:** vivid dancer damselfly

**Trees:** single-leaf piñon, bristlecone pine

## LANDMARKS AND PLACES OF INTEREST

Las Vegas

Lake Tahoe

Fly Geyser

Great Basin National Park

Red Rock Canyon

Pinball Hall of Fame

Rhyolite (ghost town)

Berlin-Ichthyosaur State Park

Hoover Dam *(see also Arizona)*

Area 51

Devils Hole

Lake Mead

## TRADITIONS AND EVENTS

Burning Man

National Elko Basque Festival

Milky Way (viewing of)

## PEOPLE

Wayne Newton

## INVENTIONS

hard hat

slot machine (Liberty Bell)

Bradley watch (named for blind Paralympic
　　athlete and Nevadan Bradley Snyder)

## CULTURAL CONTRIBUTIONS

Washoe basket

## WILDLIFE

jaguars (small population in state)

NO. 37

western meadowlark

goldenrod

THE AGATE FOSSIL BEDS

THE LIED JUNGLE

KOLACHE festival

9-1-1

FRUIT SMACK

Kool-Aid

"ARCHIE"

CHIMNEY ROCK

WORLD'S LARGEST PORCH SWING

SCOTTS BLUFF

NEBRASKA

The Cornhusker State

BUFFALO BILL CODY

PONY EXPRESS

CENTER PIVOT IRRIGATION

ARBOR day

LINCOLN

COTTONWOOD

REUBEN sandwich

CARHENGE

PANORAMA POINT

5424

CHANNEL CATFISH

STROBE light

# NEBRASKA

37TH STATE

*(entered the Union on March 1, 1867)*

**Capital:** Lincoln
**Nickname:** The Cornhusker State
**Motto:** "Equality before the Law"

## STATE SYMBOLS

**Bird:** Western meadowlark
**Fish:** channel catfish
**Flower:** goldenrod
**Insect:** honeybee
**Mammal:** white-tailed deer
**Tree:** cottonwood

## LANDMARKS AND PLACES OF INTEREST

The Agate Fossil Beds

Chimney Rock

Scott Bluffs

Archie (largest woolly mammoth fossil)

Carhenge

Panorama Point

World's Largest Porch Swing

The Lied Jungle

Niobrara State Park

## TRADITIONS AND EVENTS

Kolache Festival

## PEOPLE

Buffalo Bill Cody

Fred Astaire

## INVENTIONS

911 emergency system

Kool-Aid

Reuben sandwich

strobe light

center pivot irrigation

## FAMOUS FIRSTS

Arbor Day

## INDUSTRY

crops (alfalfa hay)

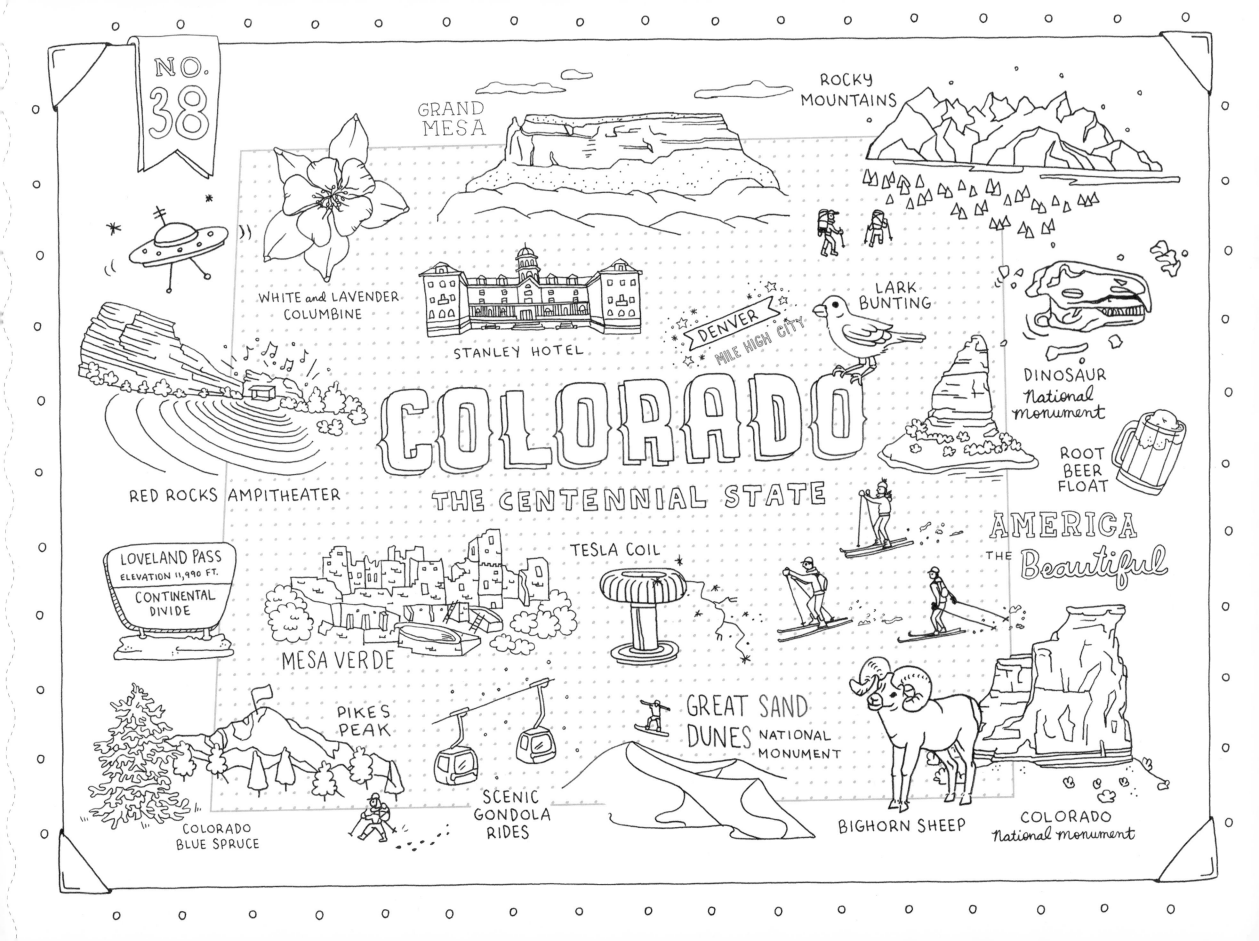

# COLORADO

## 38TH STATE

*(entered the Union on August 1, 1876)*

**Capital:** Denver (Mile High City)
**Nicknames:** The Centennial State,
    Colorful Colorado
**Motto:** "Nil Sine Numine"
    ("Nothing without Providence")

### STATE SYMBOLS

**Bird:** lark bunting
**Fish:** greenback cutthroat trout
**Flower:** columbine
**Insect:** Colorado hairstreak butterfly
**Mammal:** Rocky Mountain bighorn sheep
**Tree:** Colorado blue spruce

### LANDMARKS AND PLACES OF INTEREST

Rocky Mountains
Grand Mesa
Red Rocks Ampitheatre
Pikes Peak
Dinosaur National Monument
Great Sand Dunes National Monument
Mesa Verde
Colorado National Monument
Loveland Pass
Stanley Hotel

### TRADITIONS AND EVENTS

Denver Broncos
UFO sightings

### INVENTIONS

Tesla Coil
root beer float
    (originally called the Black Cow)
Jolly Ranchers
shredded wheat cereal

### CULTURAL CONTRIBUTIONS

"America the Beautiful" by Katharine Lee
    Bates (inspired by a trip to Pikes Peak)

### INDUSTRY

beer breweries
legal marijuana

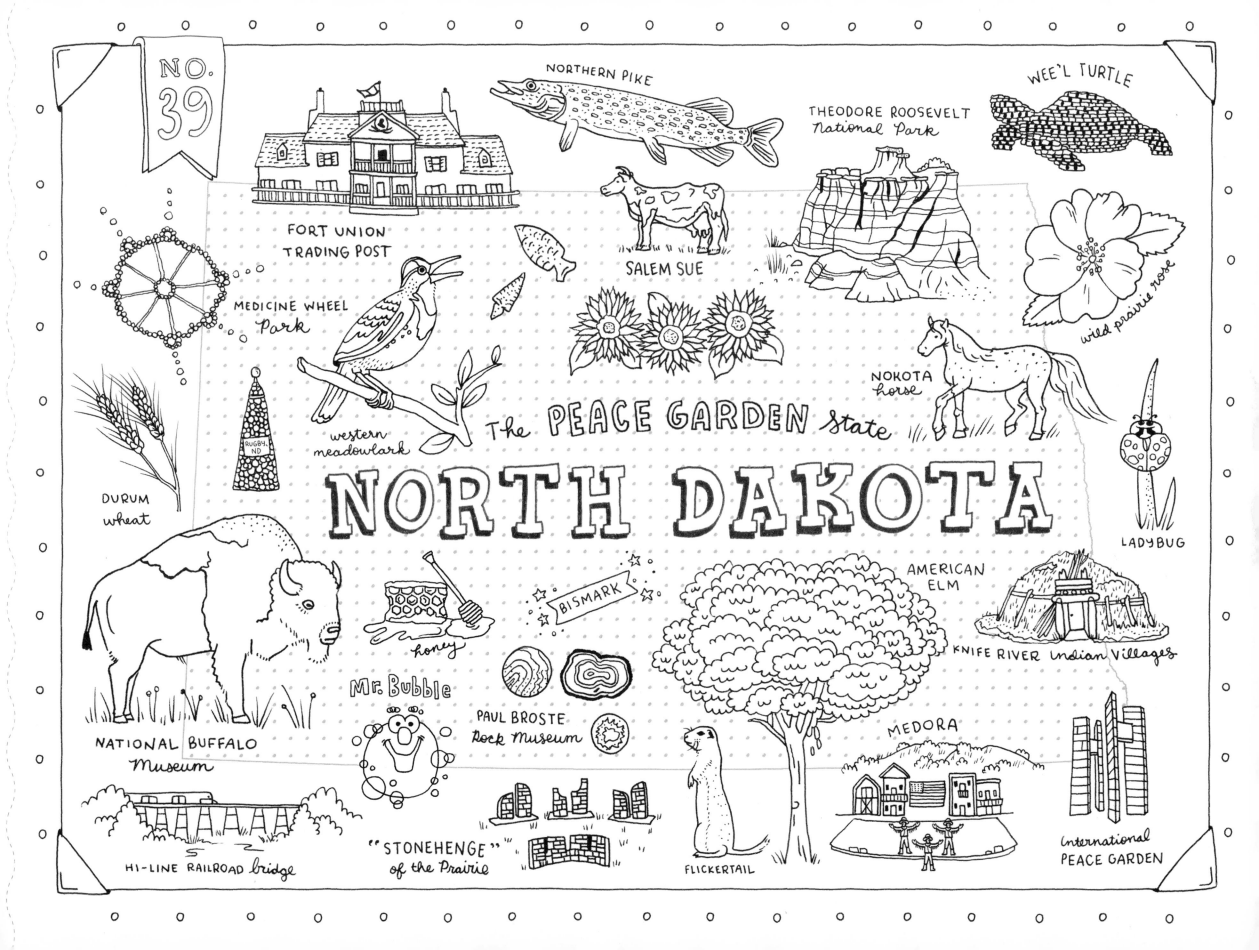

NO. 39

NORTHERN PIKE

WEE'L TURTLE

THEODORE ROOSEVELT *National Park*

FORT UNION TRADING POST

SALEM SUE

*wild prairie rose*

MEDICINE WHEEL *Park*

RUGBY, ND

*western meadowlark*

NOKOTA *horse*

The PEACE GARDEN *state*

DURUM *wheat*

LADYBUG

# NORTH DAKOTA

BISMARK

AMERICAN ELM

*honey*

Mr. Bubble

PAUL BROSTE *Rock Museum*

KNIFE RIVER *Indian Villages*

NATIONAL BUFFALO *Museum*

MEDORA

HI-LINE RAILROAD *bridge*

"STONEHENGE" *of the Prairie*

FLICKERTAIL

*International* PEACE GARDEN

# NORTH DAKOTA

39TH STATE

*(entered the Union on November 2, 1889)*

**Capital:** Bismarck

**Nicknames:** The Peace Garden State,
The Flickertail State, The Roughrider State

**Motto:** Liberty and Union Now and Forever,
One and Inseparable

## STATE SYMBOLS

**Bird:** Western meadowlark

**Fish:** Northern pike

**Flower:** wild prairie rose

**Insect:** ladybug

**Tree:** American elm

## LANDMARKS AND PLACES OF INTEREST

Theodore Roosevelt National Park

International Peace Garden

National Buffalo Museum

Fort Union Trading Post

Medicine Wheel Park

Knife River Indian Villages

High Line Bridge

"Stonehenge" of the prairie (*Mystical Horizons*)

Medora

Salem Sue (world's largest statue
of a Holstein cow)

Wee'l Turtle

Geographical Center of North America
(Rugby, ND)

Paul Broste Rock Museum

Casselton Can Pile

*Geese in Flight* sculpture (Enchanted Highway)

Lake Sakakawea

Frontier Village and World's Largest Buffalo
(statue)

## TRADITIONS AND EVENTS

Norsk Hostfest

NDSU Bison football

## PEOPLE

Lawrence Welk

Roger Maris

## INVENTIONS

Mr. Bubble

## CULTURAL CONTRIBUTIONS

*Fargo*

## WILDLIFE

Nokota horses

flickertails

## INDUSTRY

oil

crops and livestock (cattle, durum wheat)

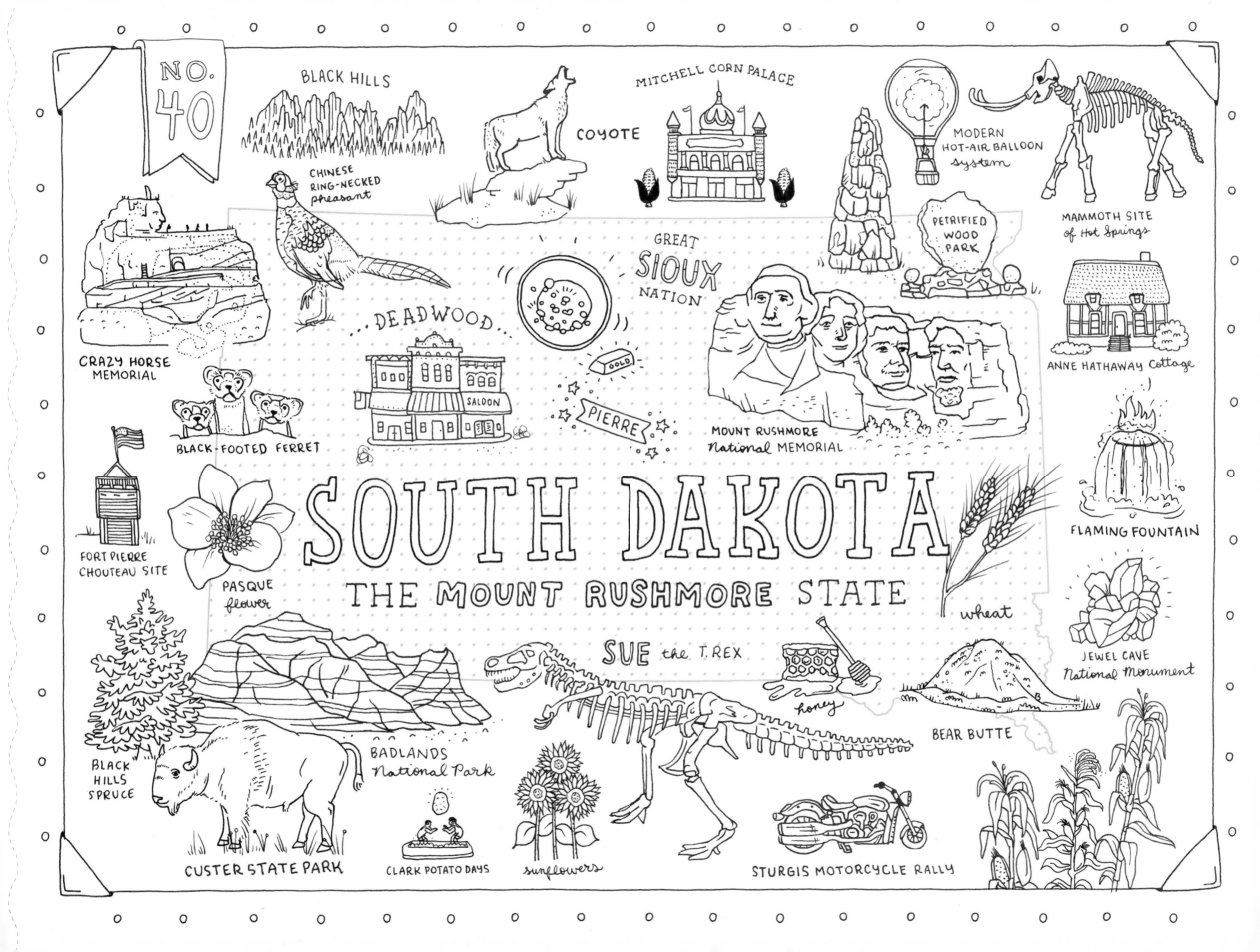

# SOUTH DAKOTA

40<sup>TH</sup> STATE

*(entered the Union on November 2, 1889)*

**Capital:** Pierre

**Nicknames:** The Mount Rushmore State, The Coyote State, Great Faces. Great Places.

**Motto:** "Under God the People Rule"

## STATE SYMBOLS

**Animal:** coyote

**Bird:** Chinese ring-necked pheasant

**Fish:** walleye

**Flower:** pasque flower

**Insect:** honeybee

**Tree:** Black Hills spruce

## LANDMARKS AND PLACES OF INTEREST

Mount Rushmore National Memorial

Crazy Horse Memorial

Mitchell Corn Palace

Badlands National Park

Sue the T. rex

Black Hills

Jewel Cave National Monument

Petrified Wood Park

Fort Pierre Chouteau Site

Deadwood

Mammoth Site of Hot Springs

Flaming Fountain

Bear Butte

Anne Hathaway Cottage

Custer State Park

## TRADITIONS AND EVENTS

Sturgis Motorcycle Rally

Clark Potato Days (includes Mashed Potato Wrestling)

## PEOPLE

Sitting Bull

Tom Brokaw

## INVENTIONS

modern hot-air balloon system

## CULTURAL CONTRIBUTIONS

Great Sioux Nation

## WILDLIFE

black-footed ferret

## INDUSTRY

crops and livestock (hay, sunflowers, rye, honey, soybeans, corn, wheat, cattle)

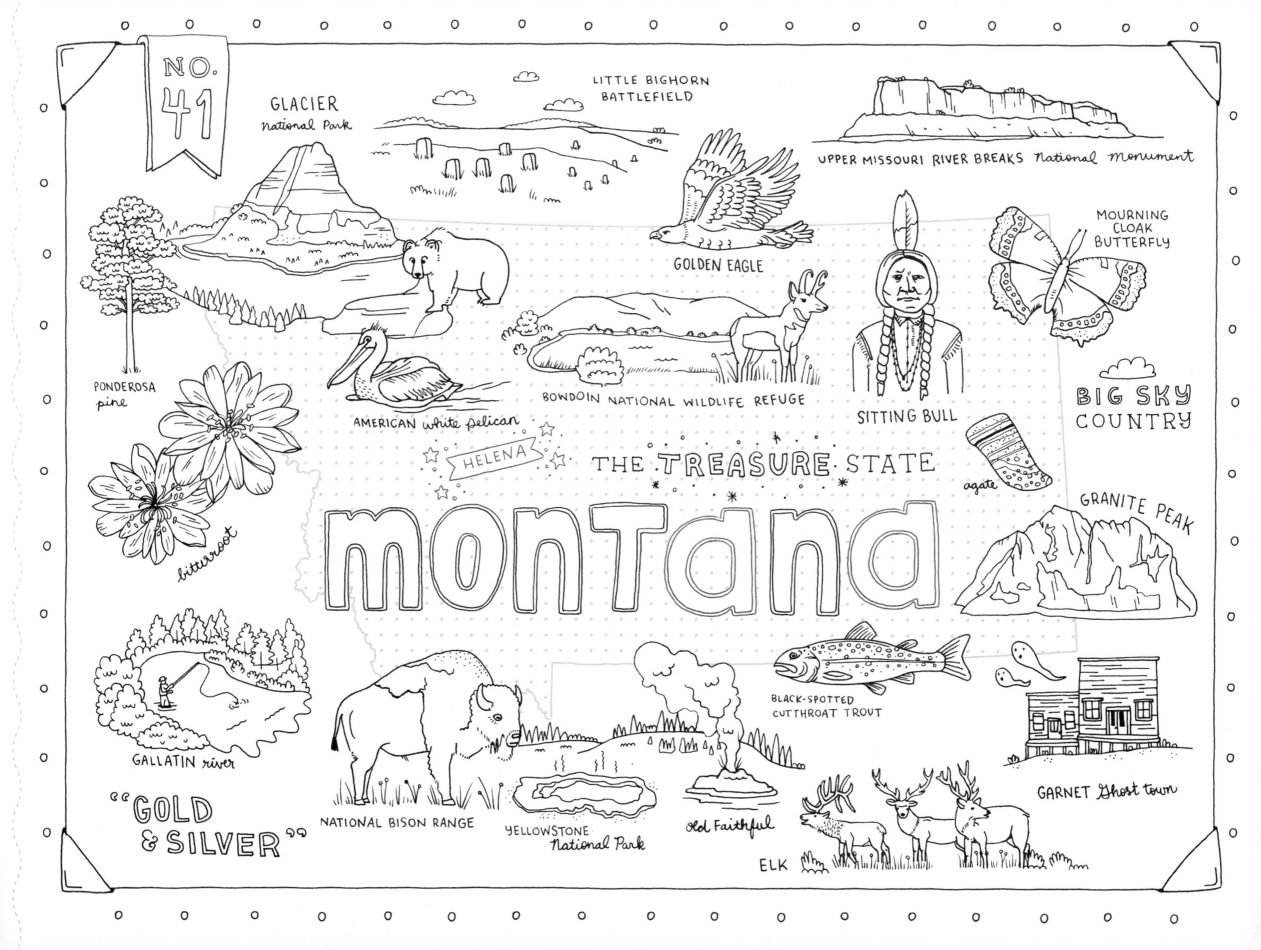

# monTana

41ST STATE

*(entered the Union on November 8, 1889)*

**Capital:** Helena

**Nicknames:** The Treasure State,
  Big Sky Country

**Motto:** "Oro y Plata" ("Gold and Silver")

## STATE SYMBOLS

**Animal:** grizzly bear

**Bird:** Western meadowlark

**Butterfly:** mourning cloak

**Animal:** grizzly bear

**Fish:** black-spotted cutthroat trout

**Flower:** bitterroot

**Gemstones:** agate and sapphire

**Tree:** ponderosa pine

## LANDMARKS AND PLACES OF INTEREST

Glacier National Park

National Bison Range

Bowdoin National Wildlife Refuge

Granite Peak

Upper Missouri River Breaks
  National Monument

Little Bighorn Battlefield

Garnet (ghost town)

Gallatin River

Yellowstone National Park
  *(see also Wyoming)*

Garden of One Thousand Buddhas

Steer Montana (world's second largest
  steer; *see also Old Ben in Indiana*)

Going-to-the-Sun Road

## TRADITIONS AND EVENTS

Crow Fair

## PEOPLE

Sitting Bull

## WILDLIFE

golden eagle

moose

elk

pronghorn antelope

American white pelican

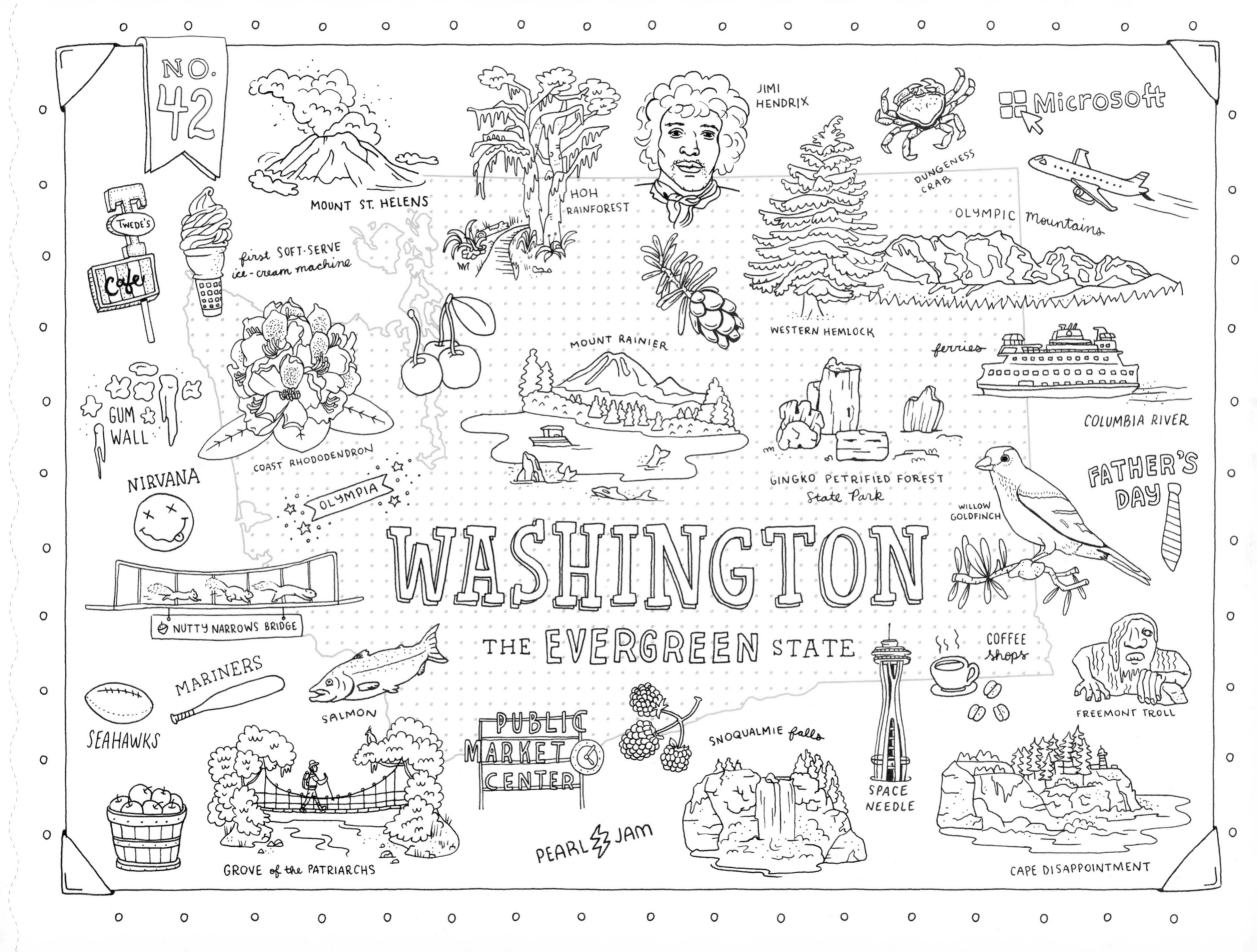

# WASHINGTON

42ND STATE

*(entered the Union on November 11, 1889)*

**Capital:** Olympia

**Nicknames:** The Evergreen State, The Green Tree State

**Motto:** "Al-ki" ("Bye and Bye")

### STATE SYMBOLS

**Bird:** willow goldfinch

**Fish:** steelhead trout

**Flower:** coast rhododendron

**Insect:** green darner dragonfly

**Mammal (endemic):** Olympic marmot

**Mammal (marine):** orca

**Tree:** Western hemlock

### LANDMARKS AND PLACES OF INTEREST

Olympic Mountains

Cape Disappointment

Nutty Narrows Bridge

Ginkgo Petrified Forest State Park

Space Needle

Mount Rainier

Grove of the Patriarchs

Snoqualmie Falls

Hoh Rainforest

Mount St. Helens

Pike Place Market

Columbia River

Gum Wall

Fremont Troll

Twede's Cafe (*Twin Peaks*)

Puget Sound

Grand Coulee Dam

### TRADITIONS AND EVENTS

sports teams (Seattle Seahawks, Mariners)

### PEOPLE

Bing Crosby

Jimi Hendrix

### INVENTIONS

Father's Day

### FAMOUS FIRSTS

soft-serve ice-cream machine

### CULTURAL CONTRIBUTIONS

grunge music

coffee shops

Twilight series (takes place in Forks, WA)

### INDUSTRY

Microsoft

Boeing

crops (largest US producer of apples, raspberries, sweet cherries)

seafood (salmon, Dungeness crabs)

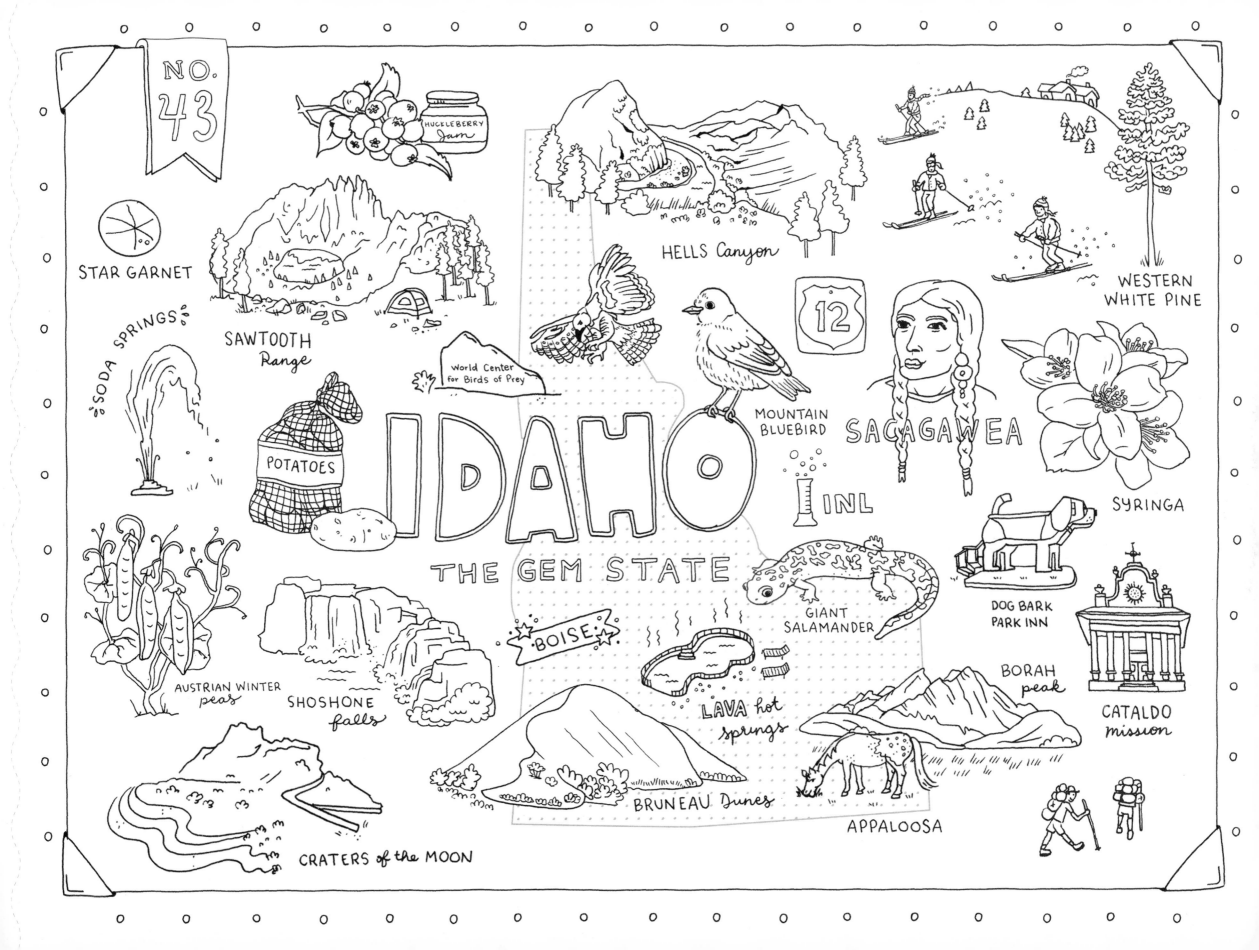

NO. 43

HUCKLEBERRY Jam

STAR GARNET

SAWTOOTH Range

SODA SPRINGS

POTATOES

World Center for Birds of Prey

HELLS Canyon

12

WESTERN WHITE PINE

MOUNTAIN BLUEBIRD

SACAGAWEA

SYRINGA

IDAHO

THE GEM STATE

INL

AUSTRIAN WINTER peas

SHOSHONE falls

BOISE

GIANT SALAMANDER

DOG BARK PARK INN

BORAH peak

CATALDO mission

LAVA hot springs

BRUNEAU Dunes

APPALOOSA

CRATERS of the MOON

# IDAHO

**43RD STATE**

*(entered the Union July 3, 1890)*

**Capital:** Boise

**Nickname:** The Gem State

**Motto:** "Esto Perpetua"
("Let It Be Perpetual"
or "It Is Forever")

## STATE SYMBOLS

**Amphibian:** Idaho giant salamander

**Bird:** mountain bluebird

**Fish:** cutthroat trout

**Flower:** syringa

**Fruit:** wild huckleberry

**Gem:** star garnet

**Horse:** Appaloosa

**Insect:** monarch butterfly

**Tree:** Western white pine

## LANDMARKS AND PLACES OF INTEREST

Sawtooth Range

Soda Springs

Hells Canyon

World Center for Birds of Prey

Cataldo Mission

Dog Bark Park Inn

Lava Hot Springs

Bruneau Dunes

Shoshone Falls

Craters of the Moon

Idaho National Laboratory

US Highway 12
(Lewis and Clark Highway)

Sun Valley

Elk River

champion Western red cedar tree

## PEOPLE

Sacagawea

## INDUSTRY

crops (potatoes, Austrian
winter peas, lentils)

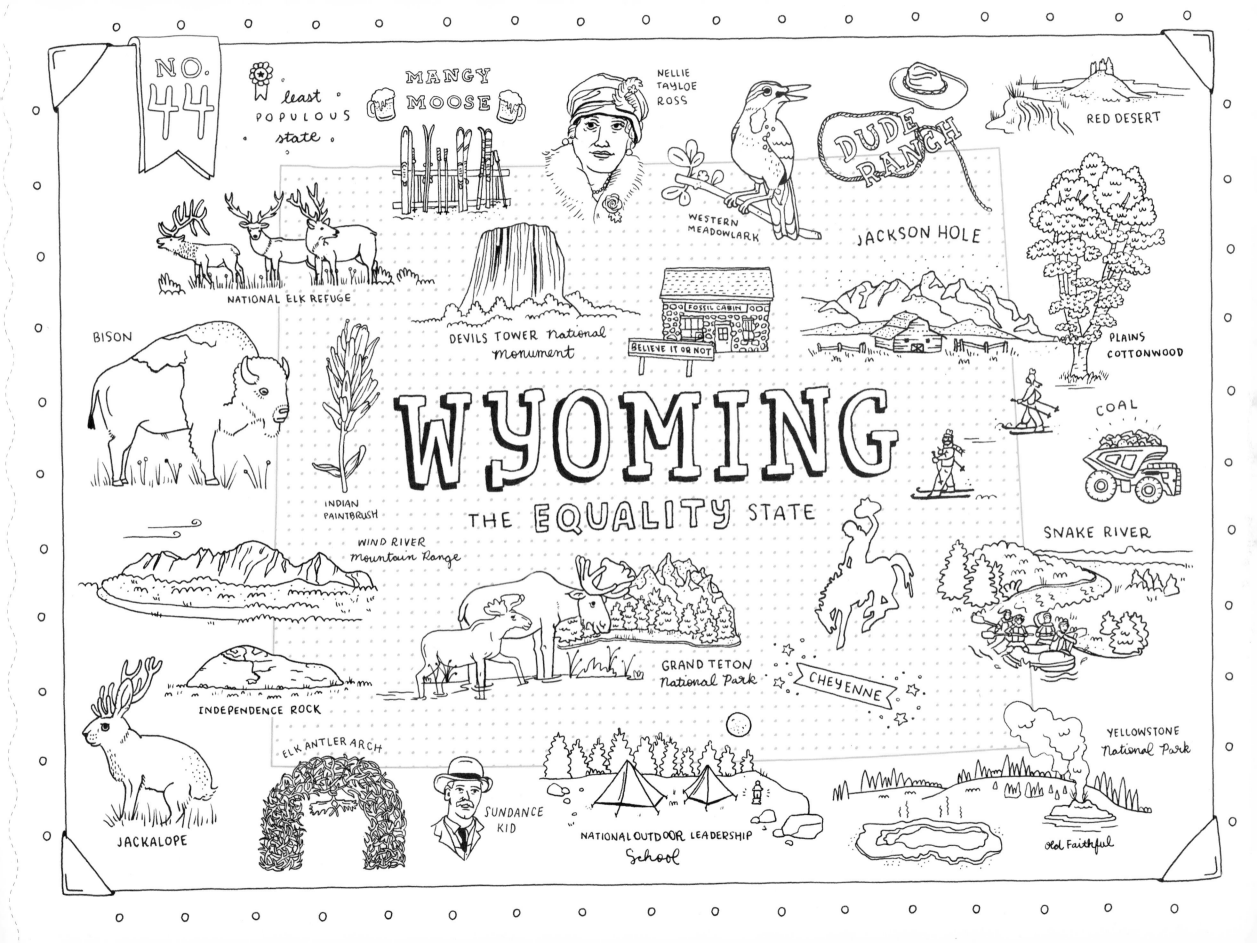

# WYOMING

## 44TH STATE

*(entered the Union on July 10, 1890)*

**Capital:** Cheyenne
**Nicknames:** The Equality State,
    The Cowboy State, Big Wyoming
**Motto:** "Equal Rights"

### STATE SYMBOLS

**Bird:** Western meadowlark
**Flower:** Indian paintbrush
**Insect:** Sheridan's green hairstreak
    butterfly
**Mammal:** bison
**Tree:** plains cottonwood

### LANDMARKS AND PLACES OF INTEREST

Devils Tower National Monument
Grand Teton National Park
Yellowstone National Park
    *(see also Montana)*
Elk Antler Arch
Independence Rock
Red Desert
Fossil Cabin
Snake River
Wind River Mountain Range
Jackson Hole
Mangy Moose
National Elk Refuge
World's Largest Jackalope

### PEOPLE

Sundance Kid

### FAMOUS FIRSTS

to allow women to vote
female US governor
    (Nellie Tayloe Ross)
dude ranch (Eatons' Ranch)

### CULTURAL CONTRIBUTIONS

National Outdoor Leadership School
    (NOLS)

### INDUSTRY

coal

# UTAH

45TH STATE

*(entered the Union on January 4, 1896)*

**Capital:** Salt Lake City
**Nicknames:** The Beehive State,
    The Salt Lake State, The Mormon State
**Motto:** "Industry"

## STATE SYMBOLS

**Animal:** Rocky Mountain elk
**Bird:** California seagull
**Cooking pot:** Dutch oven
**Fish:** Bonneville cutthroat trout
**Flower:** sego lily
**Insect:** honeybee
**Snack:** Jell-O
**Tree:** quaking aspen

## LANDMARKS AND PLACES OF INTEREST

Bonneville Salt Flats
Arches National Park
Great Salt Lake
Rainbow Bridge
Heber Valley Railroad
Bingham Canyon
Pando
Salt Lake Temple
Little Hollywood (Kanab, UT)
Cleveland-Lloyd Dinosaur Quarry
Utahraptor

## TRADITIONS AND EVENTS

Sundance Film Festival

## PEOPLE

Butch Cassidy

## INVENTIONS

Television
fry sauce

## FAMOUS FIRSTS

department store (in the US)

## CULTURAL CONTRIBUTIONS

filming locations for Westerns

## INDUSTRY

rubber chickens

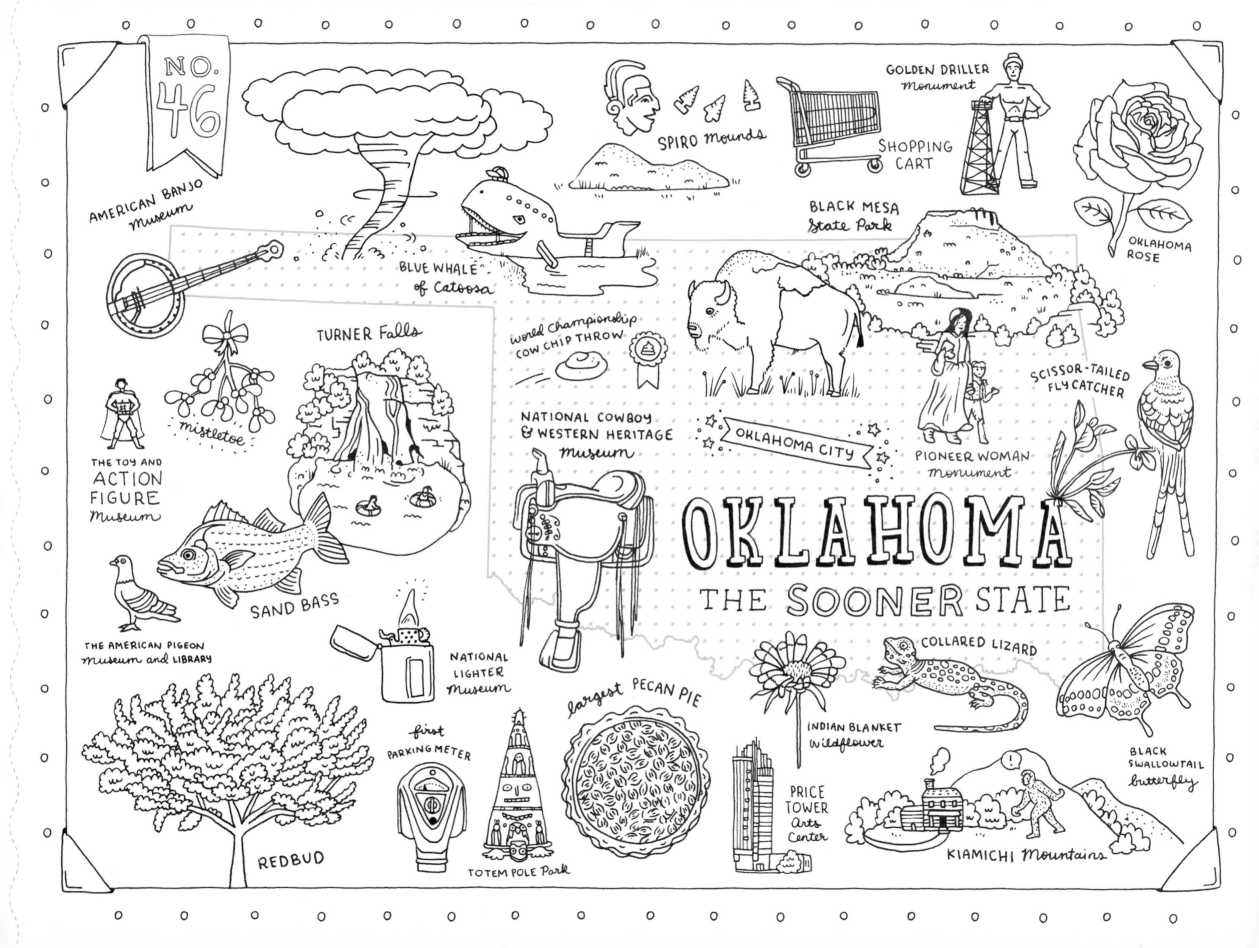

NO. 46

AMERICAN BANJO Museum

SPIRO Mounds

GOLDEN DRILLER Monument

SHOPPING CART

OKLAHOMA ROSE

BLUE WHALE of Catoosa

BLACK MESA State Park

TURNER Falls

mistletoe

THE TOY AND ACTION FIGURE Museum

World Championship COW CHIP THROW

NATIONAL COWBOY & WESTERN HERITAGE museum

OKLAHOMA CITY

PIONEER WOMAN Monument

SCISSOR-TAILED FLY CATCHER

OKLAHOMA
THE SOONER STATE

SAND BASS

THE AMERICAN PIGEON museum and LIBRARY

NATIONAL LIGHTER Museum

largest PECAN PIE

COLLARED LIZARD

INDIAN BLANKET Wildflower

BLACK SWALLOWTAIL butterfly

REDBUD

first PARKING METER

TOTEM POLE Park

PRICE TOWER Arts Center

KIAMICHI Mountains

# OKLAHOMA

46TH STATE

*(entered the Union on November 16, 1907)*

**Capital:** Oklahoma State

**Nickname:** The Sooner State

**Motto:** "Labor Omnia Vincit"
("Labor Conquers All Things")

## STATE SYMBOLS

**Animal:** buffalo

**Bird:** scissor-tailed flycatcher

**Butterfly:** black swallowtail

**Fish:** sand bass

**Floral emblem:** mistletoe

**Flower:** Oklahoma rose

**Insect:** honeybee

**Reptile:** collared lizard

**Tree:** redbud

**Wildflower:** Indian blanket

## LANDMARKS AND PLACES OF INTEREST

Golden Driller monument

Price Tower Arts Center

Totem Pole Park

The American Pigeon Museum & Library

Blue Whale of Catoosa

American Banjo Museum

National Cowboy & Western
Heritage Museum

Spiro Mounds

The Toy and Action Figure Museum

Turner Falls

Kiamichi Mountains

Black Mesa State Park

Pioneer Woman monument

National Lighter Museum

## TRADITIONS AND EVENTS

World Championship Cow Chip Throw

world record for world's largest pie

## PEOPLE

Will Rogers

## INVENTIONS

shopping cart

electric guitar

## FAMOUS FIRSTS

parking meter

yield sign

Girl Scout cookies (first sold in OK)

# NEW MEXICO

47TH STATE

*(entered the Union on January 6, 1912)*

**Capital:** Santa Fe

**Nickname:** The Land of Enchantment

**Motto:** "Crescit Eundo" ("It Grows as It Goes")

## STATE SYMBOLS

**Amphibian:** New Mexico spadefoot

**Bird:** greater roadrunner

**Butterfly:** Sandia hairstreak

**Fish:** Rio Grande cutthroat trout

**Flower:** soaptree yucca

**Insect:** tarantula hawk

**Mammal:** American black bear

**Tree:** piñon pine

## LANDMARKS AND PLACES OF INTEREST

Petroglyph National Monument

Roswell UFO Museum

Trinity Site

Georgia O'Keeffe Museum

Wheelwright Museum of the American Indian

White Sands National Monument

Carlsbad Caverns

Mining Museum

American International Rattlesnake Museum

NFO Windharp (world's largest Aeolian Harp)

Enchanted Mesa

Museum of Space History

Santa Fe Opera

Indian Pueblo Cultural Center

Aztec Ruins National Monument

Loretto Chapel "miraculous staircase"

Palace of the Governors

ABQ BioPark

Sandia Peak Tramway

Conchas Lake State Parks

*The Lightning Field*

## TRADITIONS AND EVENTS

Hatch Chile Festival

Albuquerque International Balloon Festival

World Championship Shovel Races

## INVENTIONS

breakfast burrito

## CULTURAL CONTRIBUTIONS

Smokey Bear

Laguna Pueblo pottery

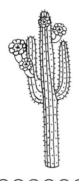

# ARIZONA

48TH STATE

*(entered the Union on February 14, 1912)*

**Capital:** Phoenix

**Nickname:** The Grand Canyon State, The Valentine State

**Motto:** "Ditat Deus" ("God Enriches")

## STATE SYMBOLS

**Bird:** cactus wren

**Butterfly:** two-tailed swallowtail

**Fish:** Apache trout

**Flower:** saguaro cactus blossom

**Mammal:** ringtail

**Neckwear:** bola tie

**Reptile:** ridge-nosed rattlesnake

**Tree:** paloverde

## LANDMARKS AND PLACES OF INTEREST

Monument Valley

London Bridge

Humphreys Peak

Hoover Dam *(see also Nevada)*

Lowell Observatory

Havasupai Falls

Carefree Sundial

Grand Canyon

Colorado River

Red Rock State Park

Tombstone

Colossal Cave

Taliesin West

Antelope Canyon

Jerome

## TRADITIONS AND EVENTS

World's Oldest Rodeo

## CULTURAL CONTRIBUTIONS

Kachina doll

## WILDLIFE

jackrabbits

coyotes

pronghorn antelope

scorpions

javelinas

## INDUSTRY

5 Cs (copper, cattle, citrus, cotton, climate)

# ALASKA

49TH STATE

*(entered the Union on January 3, 1959)*

**Capital:** Juneau

**Nickname:** The Last Frontier

**Motto:** "North to the Future"

## STATE SYMBOLS

**Bird:** willow ptarmigan

**Fish:** king salmon

**Flower:** forget-me-not

**Insect:** four-spot skimmer dragonfly

**Mammal (land):** moose

**Mammal (marine):** bowhead whale

**Tree:** Sitka spruce

## LANDMARKS AND PLACES OF INTEREST

Kodiak Island

Tongass National Forest

Katmai National Park

Denali

North Pole

Yukon River

## TRADITIONS AND EVENTS

Iditarod

blanket toss

Northern Lights

## INVENTIONS

ULU knife

## WILDLIFE

polar bears

brown bears

caribou

bald eagles

whales

## INDUSTRY

oil

seafood

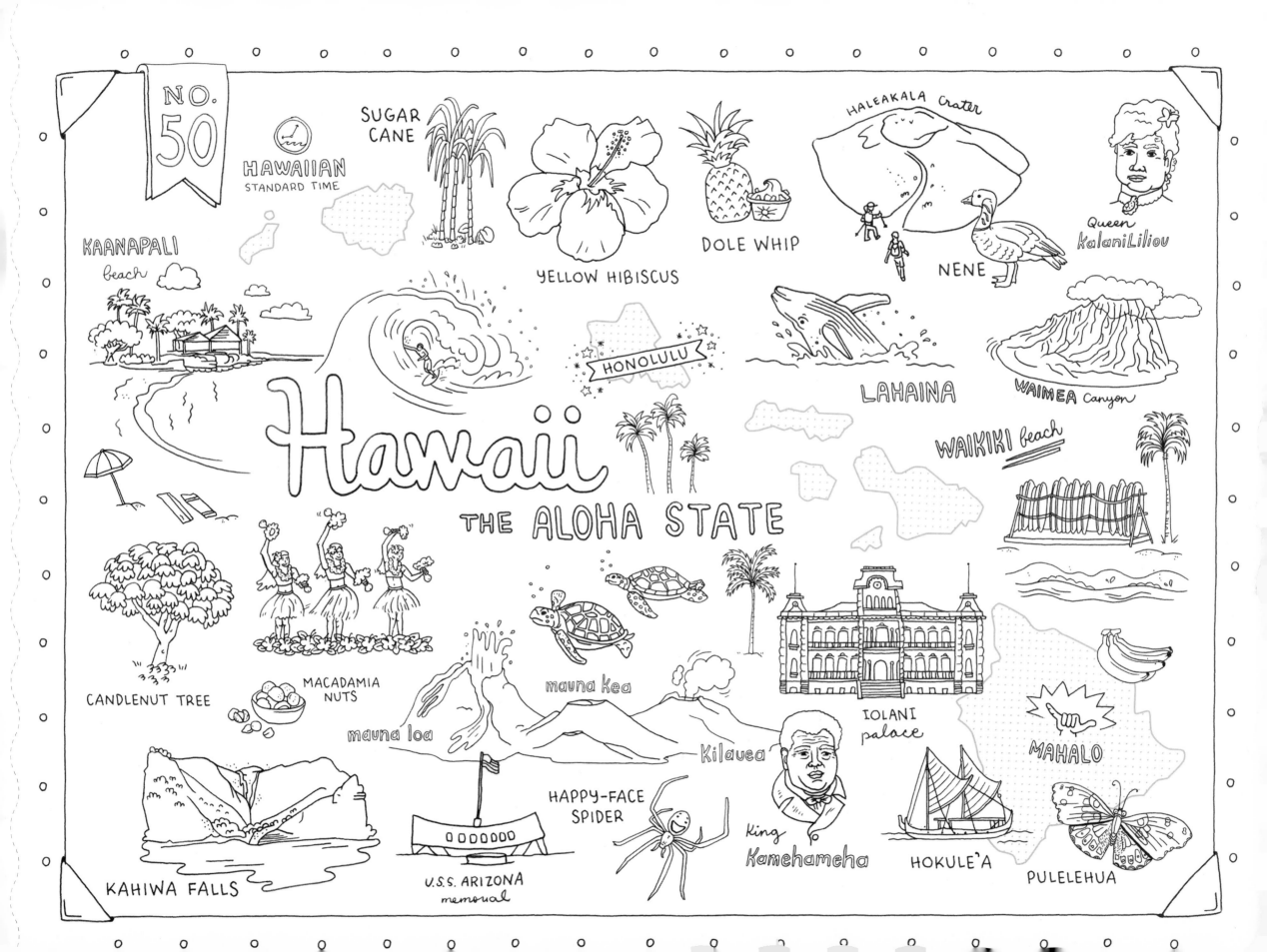

# Hawaii

50TH STATE

*(entered the Union August 21, 1959)*

**Capital:** Honolulu

**Nicknames:** The Aloha State,
The Pineapple State

**Motto:** "Ua mau ke ea o ka aina i ka
pono" ("The life of the land is
perpetuated in righteousness")

## STATE SYMBOLS

**Bird:** nene (Hawaiian goose)

**Dance:** hula

**Fish:** reef triggerfish

**Flower:** yellow hibiscus

**Insect:** pulelehua
(Kamehameha butterfly)

**Mammal:** Hawaiian monk seal

**Mammal (marine):** humpback whale

**Tree:** candlenut tree

## LANDMARKS AND PLACES OF INTEREST

Kaanapali Beach

Kahina Falls

USS *Arizona* Memorial

Mauna Loa

Mauna Kea

Kilauea

Waikiki Beach

Waimea Canyon

Haleakala Crater

Iolani Palace

Lahaina

Wailua River

Hanalei River

## TRADITIONS AND EVENTS

luau

## PEOPLE

Queen Liliuokalani

King Kamehameha

## INVENTIONS

Dole whip

shave ice

poke

## INDUSTRY

crops (pineapples, bananas,
macadamia nuts, sugar cane,
coffee, cocoa, vanilla beans,
orchids)